Defending
Christianity

unDefending Christianity

Dillon Burroughs

HARVEST HOUSE PUBLISHERS

EUGENE, OREGON

Cover design by Left Coast Design, Portland, Oregon

Published in association with the literary agency of Alive Communications, Inc., 7680 Goddard Street, Ste #200, Colorado Springs, CO 80920. www.alivecommunications.com.

In many cases, names and minor details have been changed in the real-life stories shared in this book to protect the privacy of the individuals mentioned. Where individuals may be identifiable, they have granted the author and the publisher the right to use their names, stories, and/or facts of their lives in all manners, including composite or altered representations.

UNDEFENDING CHRISTIANITY
Copyright © 2011 by Dillon Burroughs
Published by Harvest House Publishers
Eugene, Oregon 97402
www.harvesthousepublishers.com

Library of Congress Cataloging-in-Publication Data
    Burroughs, Dillon.
    Undefending Christianity / Dillon Burroughs.
      p. cm.
    ISBN 978-0-7369-3702-3 (pbk.)
    1. Christian life. I. Title.
    BV4501.3.B874 2011
    248.4—dc22

                                     2010022204

Contents

Author's Note

I used to think my job was to prove Christianity right and everyone else's religion wrong. Then I discovered Jesus didn't do this at all.

He told stories. He forgave people. He loved people.

Then I began to imagine: What would happen if I stopped arguing with people and just told stories? And listened? And showed mercy?

That's where my story begins...

Friend of Sinners, King of Beers

*Jesus was a friend to sinners and consumed
alcohol. How'd that work?*

As a kid, I was strictly taught alcohol was evil. My dad struggled with this demon for over a decade, nearly wrecking his marriage and our family in the process. He found God, dumped his Anheuser-Busch down the drain, quit smoking, and never looked back. He told me if I loved God or didn't want to visit Him in the near future, I would never touch a drink of the stuff.

I was three.

So I didn't. I am 34 years old as I type these words and have never tasted a sip of alcohol.

But when I read the Gospels, I've noticed that my dad's biblical paraphrase about alcohol being evil is slightly off. In fact, the first miracle Jesus performed was instant winemaking. No wonder people loved Him! He probably received a bunch of wedding invitations after that one.

Passover was observed with wine too. Since there was no refrigeration, nearly everyone in Jewish culture drank wine.

Then there's Communion, also known as the Eucharist, the Lord's Supper, wafer-and-juicy-juice, or whatever your particular tradition calls it. The modern practice is far different from the first time Jesus shared communion. He handed out flat bread and wine, not crackers and juice. I don't know about you, but this sounds far more appealing to me.

Imagine a church actually doing this! "This morning, we will ask the ushers to pass around the tortillas and wine. Please wait until everyone has received theirs, and then we will enjoy them together." This sounds more like chipotle than church.

What people tell us in the Bible and what really *is* in the Bible is not always the same. This is why reading Scripture is one of the most important spiritual practices a person can develop.

Ask the people who lived in Berea when the apostle Paul arrived. Paul talked about Jesus as the Messiah. The Bereans looked up the verses he mentioned from the Jewish prophets to see if he was making his story up or not. They were the kind of people who would google your name after meeting you. When they discovered Paul was on target, some of the people believed his message. A new community of believers formed. We call this the church.

Wine. Church. Now add a little music...

In high school, God became real. He was real before, but I had my doubts. I had accepted and rejected Him several times, sometimes on the same day, because life seemed more adventurous when I could do whatever I wanted.

That was before doing whatever I wanted sucked.

At 17, I had been dumped by a girl I really liked. Nothing hurts more than getting dumped. Except maybe getting hit by a flying steak, but unlike Napoleon Dynamite, I haven't experienced that one, so I can't comment. Anyway, life was not fun at this point, so I decided to make it fun. After various failed attempts, I realized that doing whatever I wanted while also trying to believe Jesus is God simply does not work. I had to choose one or the other.

So I chose Jesus.

It sounds easy—I chose Jesus—but it was the toughest decision I have ever made. All of my plans and dreams died that day. I wanted to do something significant: Perhaps I could have become a big-shot CEO or have gone on to defeat Tiger Woods at the Masters. I might have become a rock star or an NBA great. Or all of the above. Now all I had was Jesus...

And question marks.

But then I read that Jesus was a friend of sinners. This still bothers me. Not because Jesus was a friend of sinners (because that came in really handy in my case). It bothers me because if I'm trying to live like Jesus, that means I'm supposed to be a friend of sinners too.

At first, I thought friends of sinners were people who loved their neighbors as themselves. I would just say I love everybody, just as every Miss America contestant says she wishes for world peace. Case closed.

But I was wrong. When Jesus was called a friend of sinners, it was because He spent time with people the culture thought were the "real" sinners—the sinners with a capital S. You know who I'm talking about: prostitutes, closet Prince fans, drug addicts, Trekkies, party animals, ninjas, and parents who send their kids to public schools. We all have "lists" of people who we think are way worse sinners than everyone else.

In Jesus' day, the list included people like Matthew, who collected taxes for a non-Jewish government, and likely included extras for himself. It included Mary Magdalene, a mad woman who had been possessed by seven demons. There were also smelly fishermen, a political protestor, and at least one money-laundering traitor (Judas).

I'm convinced that if Jesus walked the streets of my town today, he wouldn't just hang out at Starbucks or shop at the Gap. He'd also drop in at a downtown pub or bar once in a while, just to say hey and talk to people. Maybe He would eat at Chili's, just as Michael does in *The Office*. He would probably be really friendly to all of those homeless people we neglect too. He'd wave and smile at kids and give directions to the tourists.

Actually, if you look closely, the only people Jesus was really mean to in the Gospels were the religious people. (He also spoke bluntly to Peter a time or two.) He wasn't a *How to Make Friends and Influence People* type of communicator. He would just show up, start telling stories, heal somebody, and talk about God's kingdom. The religious scholars couldn't handle this way of life. It did not compute.

But Jesus doesn't always make sense. He is God, you know. That means we can't quite understand everything He says or does. We do our best, but the Trinity is not like an ice cube or an egg, and Jesus cannot be theologized by just making up a word and calling Him the God-man (I personally prefer Superman as a theological term, but I understand this name is already trademarked.).

So maybe an occasional beer wouldn't be so wrong after all.

At least if I use it as an excuse to talk with people about God. Like people who wouldn't hang out with me to hear a sermon on Sunday morning.

Or if I'm at a wedding reception.

Or celebrating Passover with some Jewish friends.

Or communion.

Or anywhere without refrigeration.

I'm still thinking about it. Maybe I can just order coffee or drink an O'Douls next time I'm at Chili's. (Even though O'Doul's *does* contain .5 percent alcohol.) Does that count? But when it comes down to it, I don't think the alcohol is really the point.

Living as a friend of sinners is more about me intentionally loving people on their turf. Their world. I can drink a cup of water and eat Pringles, and God is pleased so long as I show His love. Unconditionally.

Plus, Starbucks is still cheaper. Barely.

Church's Chicken
Versus My Church

When you compare Church's Chicken to the contemporary
church, it looks a lot more similar than you think...

W hen I first moved to Dallas, Texas, I discovered religion was big
business. There are more megachurches, Christian universities, and
faith-based nonprofits located in the Metroplex than any other city in the
United States.

For the first time, I lived in a town with multiple Christian radio stations (in both English and Spanish). I could attend church almost any night
of the week in nearly any denomination I desired. In theory, I could have
survived off of communion bread and juice if I attended enough services.

But I also discovered that the churches in Dallas were not the only
kind of church in town. One Sunday, I heard a five-year-old boy ask his
mom if they were going to church's after church. I thought he was talking
about the second service.

I later unearthed an entire *denomination* with over 1600 locations
worldwide. Complete with fried okra, coleslaw, mashed potatoes, corn
on the cob, and honey butter biscuits, it was a new kind of "church for
the unchurched" that I had identified.

They call it Church's Chicken.

Started in 1952 in San Antonio, Texas, it serves over one billion dollars'
worth of fried chicken and related foods per year to its loyal membership
of three million people per week. It sounded wonderful! My secret initial
reaction about this unique denominational network was to wonder if they
offered the Eucharist with any of their value meals.

But as I researched www.churchschicken.com, I discovered the truth: Church's is not really a church at all; rather, it is a fast food franchise.

It just took me some time to figure it out because their website looked a lot like the other church websites I had been looking at to find a new church home.

Part of me wishes I would have found Church's Chicken a little earlier in my church search.

The truth is that there are far more similarities between many local churches and Church's Chicken than we would care to admit. For example, a quick scan of a local congregation's literature often reveals a sordid purpose-driven-church-looking-statement knockoff that rewords the Great Commission with "Helping people develop a growing relationship with Christ."

Other churches get creative and claim their mission statement is simply "Up, down, in, out," but they end up sounding more as if they're encouraging the hokey pokey, macarena, or chicken dance.

Some churches also get carried away and try to compete with the local phonebook for the longest mission statement to get into the *Guinness World Records* book, but most would fit into the "Help people know Jesus better-er" category.

Church's Chicken's mission statement? Church's Chicken's latest promotion states, "I *know* what good is!" They, too, have a mission to develop fully devoted followers of chicken.

A look at a local church menu usually includes worship services, Bible studies, a hair club for men, women's conferences, AWANA, bingo nights, Upward Sports, missionary updates, Pokémon tournaments, and the latest band touring through town.

Church's Chicken's menu? Original Chicken, Spicy Chicken, and Tender Strips made of (you guessed it) chicken.

Most church websites also include information on how to become a member with lots of details that sound like the end of a Viagra commercial. The closest equivalent at Church's Chicken is called "Nutrition Info." As with Viagra commercials, I'm scared to find out what appears in the fine print.

One feature Church's Chicken's web page includes, however, are two nifty buttons labeled "Franchising" and "Global." In other words, their website recruits chicken disciples to help them launch new fried chicken ministries around the world to fulfill the Great Chickmission.

I have clicked through hundreds of church websites and have only discovered two that include a prominent link about starting new ministries or churches somewhere else other than their own buildings.

Both churches were in Texas.

God moves in mysterious ways.

———

Two observations about the church versus Church's Chicken:

First, most churches, like Church's Chicken, communicate a *consumer* mentality that says, "Try me," "Buy me," or "Pick me." (*Shrek's* Donkey comes to mind here.) Second, Church's Chicken appears, based on its promotional material, to be much more "evangelistic" in its efforts than the vast majority of local churches.

The first observation is a paradox of sorts. The church *is* called to reach the people around them. Accommodating a consumer mind-set makes sense to accomplish this goal. But I have yet to find a verse in the New Testament emphasizing my felt needs as much as it does challenging me to transform to be more like Jesus.

Unfortunately, a banner that says "Be More Like Jesus!" on a church website doesn't help much. But is the alternative to offer all of a church's guests a free Starbucks gift card on its "Grand Opening" Sunday? (I'm not making this up! I almost drove there even though the service was seven hours away.)

Gift cards, of course, are not sinful. (I included them on my last Christmas list.) There is no Eleventh Commandment demanding, "Thou shalt not give away gift cards." But I really question whether the early church leader James would agree with this method.

He started his letter by telling his readers to consider it pure joy when life fell apart. Not even a free sticker or balloon. My daughters would not like that at all.

I think if I started a church (not a Church's Chicken, although combining the two could be interesting), I would look at the first church to figure out how to go about it.

The second observation about the church versus Church's Chicken is more convicting for me personally. In my years of working in churches, I didn't attempt to rally students or adults at my church and recruit them to start new churches. Maybe I should have. Multitudes of people at church are so underchallenged that they text message each other and update their Facebook statuses during the service more than they listen to the sermons.

What if my goal in leading a church was to actually recruit men and women to launch their own little franchises to change the world for Jesus?

In some ways, I did. I told students to share their faith and go on mission trips. I've helped students get to Africa and Asia and South America and Europe to let people know about our great God. But I never put it in terms of "starting your own movement."

I recently noticed that Campus Crusade, a really helpful organization that has nothing to do with the Crusades, put the following words on their website: "Helping Build Spiritual Movements Everywhere."

That really highlights what I'm perplexed about in this conversation. The church is *not* Church's Chicken and is called to function differently. However, we're called to be both different *and* better. Better would mean helping Christ's servants (that's us) be hands and feet and toes and belly buttons all over the globe to tell people Jesus loves them and offer meaning for their lives.

So eat at Church's Chicken, go to church, and start spiritual movements everywhere.

But what's a spiritual movement? Is it like a bowel movement or anarchy or acne or acupuncture or some other word that starts with *A*? A spiritual movement is more like what Mother Teresa did. She showed the love of Jesus to those she met. In her words, she "started with the need in front of her." It didn't matter whether the person had leprosy or drank Pepsi. She *was* a spiritual movement.

If you prefer an example beyond Mother Teresa, look at Jesus. Everywhere He walked, people followed Him. He *was* (and is) a spiritual movement. Except His movement is much bigger. We call it Christianity.

Words like *Christian* and *Christianity* are not unpopular today because of the Christ part. They're unpopular because of the "us" part. When our spiritual movements are nonexistent, or when they *do* look like bowel movements, Jesus looks bad. And so does His movement we call Christianity.

Some emergent-like reformers now argue that Christians shouldn't call themselves Christians because it's not cool and people might not like us or some other psychological crap. But instead of avoiding Christianity, Christians are called to affirm it, live it, and just do it.

Here is my confession: My name is Dillon Burroughs, and I am a Christian.

And I like Church's Chicken and starting spiritual movements.

Insert your name here if you follow Jesus: My name is _____, and I am a Christian. Say it out loud. (Unless you're reading this on the bus or in your cubicle or on an airplane or…You get the idea.)

Try it again. My name is _____, and I am a Christian.

Claim the name of Jesus and live like Him. For better or worse, richer or poorer. If you are a Christian, you *are* part of the church, Christ's bride. Time to live like it.

Hollywood and Flaming Liberals

Christians love movies and winning elections. They also love to rant against immoral Hollywood stars and call Democrats the devil.

Christians love movies. I know because I am one—a Christian, that is. I also know because I often talk with other people who call themselves Christians, and I have discovered they too watch movies. And not just the G-rated ones or videos with singing vegetables or films that start with the letter *F* such as *Flywheel, Facing the Giants, Fight Club*, or *Fireproof*. (Hint: One of these things is not like the others.)

And not just the ones that have "Jesus" in the name of the title or a dove-symbol on them, but real Hollywood movies rated PG and beyond, including my personal favorite, *Star Wars*.

Long before the invention of iTunes, I watched *Star Wars: A New Hope* as my first film in a dollar theater when I was a preschooler. I couldn't read the cool scrolling text at the beginning and forgot what happened to Greedo until I saw it again on HBO. All I remember is that Luke was cool. Darth Vader was bad. And I wanted a blue lightsaber for Christmas.

Years later, I discovered there were people who thought *Star Wars* was anti-biblical propaganda attempting to subvert young minds into eastern mysticism. I had no idea that attempting to copy Chewbacca's Wookiee growl was a secret plot to turn me against God.

How little I knew then.

This was my first introduction into the bizarre world called Christian film criticism. This fun little sub-sub-subculture has advanced to the point where I can now access Christianized film reviews even before the movie is available in theaters. Even better, there are now "Christian" films that offer alternatives to the so-called smut put out by the immoral moviemakers who control the Hollywood machine. I guess it's one of the ways Christian fundamentalists like to stick it to the man.

One popular Christian review system even ranks films based on how many times particular curse words are dropped, including comments like "three occurrences of the s-word."

But sometimes the best movies are the ones with lots of language. And I'm not talking about the Christian cusswords like *crap* or *dang*, but the real ones that kids use on the bus on the way to those God-forsaken public schools (I know because I was one).

Yes, I said it. I am an honest Christian who admits to preferring well-crafted films with cursing and violence over poorly made renditions of the life of Christ.

And so do you.

———

Why? Because film is an art form. It both reflects how culture is *and* influences how culture becomes. Christians (especially the fundamentalist ones who think Boba Fett is the devil) think exclusively about the second half of this equation. But what if we used such films as an opportunity to understand our culture and better engage in dialogue that leads people to faith?

Don't get me wrong. I don't let my kids watch *SpongeBob* or *Family Guy* for a reason. I avoid movies with lots of naked people in them. I'm even one of those super-Christians who controls what shows my kids watch. Yet I'm not ready to shut down the film industry. Why? Because of two movies:

Juno and *Bella*.

If you haven't seen both of these films, stop reading right now and order a copy of each (I'm serious!). Though radically different in approach and worldview, they highlight one common problem Christians like to rant about—abortion.

If there's one traditional, white-collar, conservative, Republican social issue that gets me fired up, it's the pro-life issue. I remember looking at my third child, Audrey, on a sonogram at the eight-month mark of my wife's pregnancy. If a beating heart, toes, and even hair (Yes, hair!) don't count for a human life, what does?

Juno takes this pragmatic PG-13 approach where its lead character, creatively named Juno, stops at a Planned-Parenthood-like clinic for an appointment. On the way in, she meets a classmate with a sign opposing abortion. At the end of their not-so-encouraging conversation, her protesting classmate tells her that her baby already "has fingernails."

Fingernails destroy Juno's plans. She can think of nothing but the fact that the baby inside her has fingernails.

In a moment of boldness, Juno runs out of the clinic and chooses to keep the child.

Bella takes a different direction on the same issue. A New York waitress discovers she is unexpectedly pregnant and plans to "take care of it." A compassionate co-worker befriends her in her time of trouble, dealing with his own haunting past in the process.

I won't tell you what happens at the end of this one, but I rarely cry during movies, and I cried more at the end of this film than I had in a long time.

Films communicate. Some better than others. If you can find a film that has more good than bad, then learn from it, listen to it, and don't tell me how it ends.

Besides, I didn't ruin the end of *Bella* for you.

(All that being said, don't watch porn. See my chapter on porn for details. My name is Dillon Burroughs, and I approve this message.)

And speaking of politics...I've read the Bible for several years now (yes, the whole thing!) and one thing I've discovered is that much of what Christians argue about regarding politics is just not in there. (Unless it's in the concordance. I have never read the concordance. Or the Apocrypha or the Lost Gospels or Satanic Bible. I'm not counting those.)

The Bible says a lot about government and political issues, but I don't see anywhere that tells me God is for or against universal health care or why I'm a horrible sinner condemned to the lowest pit of hell if I don't register to vote. (Confession: I didn't vote last year. Or the year before that. But I have before. I had a friend run for office one time. He won. Maybe I should vote again, but I don't want to jinx my perfect record.)

I have found two concepts in Scripture I do my best to apply: The first one is in the apostle Paul's first letter to Timothy. If anyone should have been furious at the government, it was Paul. He had been arrested and jailed multiple times for speaking out about Jesus. (He could have called a big-shot lawyer and made Fox News today, but instead he preached Jesus for two years under house arrest.)

Talking about Jesus was his only crime. But in the second chapter of his letter, he tells Timothy that Christians are to *pray* for their national leaders, not sue them, make fun of them, or mock them. They were not to impersonate the president or prime minister at Christian conventions and make fun of their idiosyncrasies. He just said to pray.

Prayer makes a great starting point. You want *real* change? Pray for the people who help create it.

The second idea is in another one of Paul's letters called Romans. It's way longer and much more detailed, but the main theme of the letter is that we all suck and only Jesus can change that. But here I'm only talking about the thirteenth chapter.

There we find a plea to submit to governing authorities. I think the accurate theological interpretation is to obey the law.

So pray for our leaders and obey the law. Oh, yeah, plus Jesus said to give to Caesar what is Caesar's, which is a really cool way to say that you need pay your taxes.

So pray for our leaders, pay taxes, and obey the law.

If Christians could really do these three things, we might actually make some progress. But instead, we make up some special category of sinner called *liberal* and talk about how the wrath of God is coming soon to a theater near you and that God has a special level in hell for them. That's a scam. I've seen better lies in my e-mail spam.

If Jesus showed up in America today, I don't think He'd be writing a book called *The Obama Nation* (I can't believe someone actually did this!). I seriously doubt He'd be up in arms about His 501(c)(3) status, which won't let Him call Democrats the devil during a Sunday sermon.

In fact, a while back I posted this article called "Obama Spirituality." It goes like this: As a Christian, I had never spoken out on politics. I just didn't get too fired up about it. I was more concerned about making it to church on time and taking care of my own family than stressing over which bill was bogged down in Congress.

But then someone asked me to talk on the radio about Obama and evangelicals. I said, "Sure, why not?" I had no idea what I was getting into.

I found out after accepting the interview that many Christians don't like Barack Obama. It's not because he's African American; it's because of abortion, his views on same-sex marriage, war, and a whole lot more. But then I said the Bible gave two clear concepts for relating to our president: Pray and submit.

People didn't like that. They wanted me to call Democrats the devil and lead a movement to impeach Obama and make Jesus president. But I didn't.

So now I'm the bad guy.

I get hate mail, hate Facebook-mail, hate e-mail, and hate blog comments—mostly from Christians.

Let's be honest: That just sucks. Jesus said A) love God, B) love your neighbor, and C) love your enemies. I don't consider Obama my God nor my enemy, but he's my neighbor (not literally, but I'm originally from Indiana, so close enough). So I love Barack Obama. If you're a Christian, pick options B or C and do likewise.

Then pray for him. He has a tougher job than you do, and if he does blow it, it won't help any of us. Plus, if you keep making Christians look stupid, we'll eventually become the bad guys (we often already are) and people will ignore us completely instead of listening to our ideas to make this country a better place.

You don't have to vote for someone to love them.

But if you're a Christian, you have to love Barack Obama.

Whether you like it or not.

———

But I bet Jesus would have been really angry about how the national government responded after Hurricane Katrina and would have praised the individuals, including many of His followers, who stepped in the gap to help. He would really like Habitat for Humanity, being a carpenter and all. And He would definitely like *Star Wars*.

Not just because it's rated PG. It would be because the main point of the film is that for the good guys to win, they have to face some ugly things about themselves first. Luke had to deal with his father. (All the good cowboys have daddy issues!) C3-PO had the Jawas. Even Leia had to deal with Han Solo's attitude.

Jesus would really want people who claim to follow Him to do the same. If we're going to point a finger (preferably not the tall finger) at the "bad guys" in Hollywood and the White House, we have to realize we have four fingers pointing at ourselves.

Our role models for interacting with government are not supposed to be Goliath or Ehud, but heroes like Daniel and Esther and Nehemiah. All three of these individuals feared God and served their governing leaders with respect.

And they turned out all right. All three have books in the Bible named after them.

Esther even has her own movie.

Nehemiah gets shout-outs at most of the pastor's conferences about rebuilding churches and taking the city for God and fund-raising with a sword in one hand and working with the other. John Maxwell really seems to like him too.

And Daniel has his own *Veggie Tales* episode.

He was a slave who became second-in-command in a nation that worshiped pagan gods and goddesses. Plus, he had three friends who could walk through fire.

Esther was basically turned into a concubine by her king, but she used her life to save the entire Jewish people and left us the holiday of Purim.

Nehemiah served an occupying king and prayed a lot until his boss allowed him to rebuild the city of his people in Jerusalem.

And none of these three God-followers complained about whether they could pray at a graduation, football game, or city council meeting in the name of Jesus. They just served God, prayed, and made the most of their lives in helping others.

Sounds like a plan. ☺

I Love Homosexuals
Even Though I'm Straight

Jesus said to love your neighbor, love sinners, and love your enemies.
Homosexuals should fit into at least one of these three categories.

There was this guy in my high school who sang in choir, acted in drama, and wasn't the most manly man in the world. I thought he had a great personality, and I was into music, so we hung out and were fairly close friends my senior year. The next year, I moved away to college and heard via the gossip network back home…*Insert drumroll here*…

My friend had announced to the world he was gay. This was becoming a popular act in American culture at the time, but it surprised me. We weren't best friends, but I had been to his house. We had hung out on weekends together, and we spent lots of time talking about life. I had even talked with him about his spiritual background and shared how Jesus had changed my life and could change his.

He never once mentioned he was gay. When I heard the news, I thought, *Maybe he was afraid to mention it. Maybe he wasn't gay then. Maybe…*

Then I heard the rest of the report. Because I was his friend, a nasty rumor was rapidly being disseminated that I was also officially gay. Gossip frustrates me when it's *not* about me. Now that it *was* about me and included a big stinking lie about my sexual orientation, I was furious.

I had never mentioned being homosexual. Quite the opposite, my reputation in high school included several traditional dating relationships. I was quite happy pursuing the opposite sex.

That's when I realized I had been labeled gay by association.

———

There's a similar story in the life of Jesus. He had been hanging out with prostitutes, tax collectors, and other people labeled *sinners* with a capital *S* in His society. When He did, gossip spread.

Who knows exactly what was said? The Gospel writers were kind enough to spare us the details of mudslingers who accused Jesus of having too much fun with the ladies or creating shady financial deals behind the scenes. If they hadn't, we'd probably find ourselves much angrier after reading the New Testament narratives.

But we can imagine the talk. The times change, but gossip remains the same. Jesus would have been a prostitute by association, a pimp, and a man who lived above the law.

He might have even been accused of being homosexual.

Just like me.

———

After my initial anger, it struck me that no one else in my high school was being outed as gay without claiming it for themselves. Why had I been targeted? I think it was because at that time I had helped lead a group of students who were trying to live out our faith at school. As part of my weirdness, I hugged people. Everybody. I don't do it as much now because I work in an office, and I don't like to spill everyone's coffee in the morning, but back then, I just hugged anyone and everyone.

Including my now out-of-the-closet friend.

So if showing expressions of kindness by hugging is a gay activity, go ahead and call me gay.

———

In college, I had a guy e-mail me to "confess" that he struggled with same-sex attraction as a Christian. It was the first time I had heard of this strange phenomenon, so I asked a bunch of questions and said I would pray for him. One e-mail turned into two, ten, and twenty. Then I lost count and suggested we should really meet face-to-face sometime to quit encouraging our mutual carpal tunnel.

When we finally connected, I realized he was a grad student I had met at the beginning of the semester. He was a few years older than me, and he was clearly uneasy about the situation. But because I had talked with him about same-sex attraction like any other struggle a person might have, he was willing to give our lunch a chance.

In fact, after a few opening minutes of awkwardness, we had a down-right fascinating conversation about the process of transformation as a follower of Christ and how it's not as simple as all those bestselling self-help books claim. I discovered he was even already in contact with a counselor and in the process of living a life that God's Word calls "worthy of the calling you have received."

Notice what happened: A guy chose to follow Jesus and realized he had a problem doing it. Why? Jesus has communicated that sex is designed for marriage with your partner (a future wife, in his case). He was struggling with thoughts and actions that were inconsistent with this pattern, and he was searching for help. His search led to a community with trusted individuals who could help point him in the right direction.

This not-so-thought-out plan from my college years has become my approach to homosexuality in general. If you don't follow Jesus, the guidelines of the Bible don't matter too much to you. But if you want to pursue the lifestyle Jesus communicated, same-sex activity isn't in the equation.

You deal with it like any other issue that Christians typically call sin and help people move from where they are to progressive steps closer to the cross, whether the issue is overeating, masturbation, anger, porn, hetero-, bi-, or homosexuality, or eating too many cookies. (That last one was about me.)

Another twist Jesus brings to this whole homosexuality scenario is love. *Love changes everything.* He challenged His hearers to love their neighbors, love their spouses, love their friends, and even to love their enemies. Homosexuals have to fit into one of these categories. There is no other option.

That's why our culture's media circus over same-sex marriage is doomed from the start. It's not about Christians loving homosexuals and helping them follow Jesus. Christians who stand for the Bible's perspective on marriage are labeled the bad guys. They *can't* be the ones who love. They're trying to *stop* people from loving.

The whole scenario is wrong. The issue is not even about marriage as much as it is about Christians who care about what Jesus says about life. But those who create the news don't frame the story that way.

So if same-sex marriage becomes the norm, what does that say about Christians? Are we now both the enemy *and* losers? I'd much rather focus on our calling to communicate how God has changed our lives and how He can help change the lives of others regardless of background. Part of that overarching change includes sexual orientation. When we do, we become servants and disciples with a different perspective that might actually work.

Jesus said something else about following Him that continues to haunt me on a regular basis. He told His inner circle that people would know they followed Jesus by *the love they had for one another*. Our light is to shine not only to those around us. Our love for one another must be visible enough that outsiders recognize it when they look at those weird people who believe that a Jewish rabbi walked out of a tomb and is God in human form.

I'm convinced that part of the path to impacting the gay community of our culture is to provide something they crave in their relationships only Christ can provide—real love. Since my early encounters with those involved in homosexual relationships, I've shared countless conversations with men and women of the same-sex persuasion in their quest for love. But the romantic chase continues to disappoint, and those who are honest with me share that something is still missing.

That something is love.

That love is found only in knowing God.

And knowing God can only happen through Jesus.

But those I cry for in my prayers at night will likely never give Jesus a chance unless they come across at least one individual like you or me who lives the way of Jesus. If I turn and run when I see a homosexual protester, I am not acting like Jesus. If I protest with my own signs, I am not responding like Jesus. If I belittle or criticize without offering hope, I am not speaking like Jesus. But if I show His love in every interaction to the best of my God-given abilities to both those who are like me and those who are not, someone might be changed.

That someone might be your friend. Your son. Your daughter. Your brother. Your sister. Your mom. Your dad.

That someone might even be you.

Ending Slavery Begins
with Me...and You

*More slaves exist now than any other time in human history. Even
in the U.S., you can buy people if you know where to go. The
only way to end it begins with you and me, one step at a time.*

In June 2009, I travelled to Haiti for the second time. I flew alone, meeting with a team from Texas and Oklahoma upon landing at the Port-au-Prince airport. A small circle of pastors and other church leaders introduced themselves as we waited for our contact. I knew the week would be interesting when I spotted one guy in all University of Texas orange, down to his Longhorn luggage bag, standing next to a second fellow in an Oklahoma Sooners cap.

The only person in the group near my age was a guy named Edgar. He was a bilingual youth worker from the Houston area who had experienced mission work in over 20 countries. We bunked together that week as we took part in our efforts at Mission of Hope, an inspiring work changing the lives of thousands of Haitians through their local efforts and international leadership of the humanitarian network called Haiti One.

During our evening chats, Edgar and I talked about a lot of issues, ranging from family to vocation and making a difference as husbands, dads, and followers of Christ. Upon departing, we committed to keeping in contact, with Edgar inviting me to speak to his group of teenagers the next time I was in Houston.

That November, I had made arrangements to visit some friends on the south side of Houston and was able to set up a speaking engagement at Edgar's church in the process. Edgar's pastor had graciously invited me to share with his entire congregation as part of the trip. As my Houston tour neared, I had started working on another research project related to human trafficking in the U.S., a phenomenon I knew nothing about until researching the Haitian forced child labor situation I learned about during my summer trip. At first, I thought the situation of child slavery in Haiti was unique to the developing world. Certainly, you couldn't find too many places you could buy a child for $50, could you?

To my shock, I unearthed the ugly truth that modern slave trade takes place within our borders as well. Our government estimates 14,500 to 17,500 people are trafficked into the U.S. from abroad each year for some form of forced labor, not including people forced into various forms of labor and sexual exploitation within our own borders. Once I learned this, I felt compelled to help. I joined up with another friend of mine in Atlanta named Charles, who was working in this area, and we began the hard work of connecting people, information, and resources to do something to end trafficking in our country. (I have much more to say about Charles in the next chapter.)

As I prepared for my Houston flight, Charles said I should see if there was anyone in that area I could interview on the issue of trafficking. After all, Texas is considered one of the top spots in the nation for human trafficking, with estimates that over 20 percent of trafficking victims pass through its borders. He even tracked down an organization online to forward to me as a contact.

The name of the organization was Home of Hope Texas.

On a whim, I dialed the number on my cell phone as I was worked through my list of preparations a couple of days before my flight. A guy named Mark Palmer answered the phone. The conversation was one of those God things that only make sense if you believe in Providence.

I proceeded to explain to Mark I was speaking at a church in his area that weekend and wanted to talk with him about his work to fight human trafficking. He asked where I would be speaking, and I told him the name of the church—Humble First Assembly.

"That's my church," Mark replied.

"Your church?" Houston has a population of over five million people and several thousand churches. The odds that I would speak at the church this complete stranger attends is far beyond normal. We both acknowledged something special could be in the works and set a time to have lunch after the service.

Sunday came, and we ended up at Outback Steakhouse for lunch. Only God could have arranged the combination of people at the table: two of my friends from my days of serving in the Dallas area; my friend Edgar from my Haiti trip (along with his family); and Mark and Sandra Palmer, the founders of the one Christian anti-trafficking group in the area.

Sandra Palmer's story was especially powerful. Having worked in missionary efforts her entire life, she had helped raise funds to develop a home of hope for sex slavery survivors in India with Project Rescue, led by David and Beth Grant. After visiting the home she had helped to build in India, she returned to Texas and began to discover similar tragic stories of young women forced into prostitution. An activist at heart, she soon founded Home of Hope Texas with her husband, Mark, and began work toward Houston's first long-term aftercare center for sex trafficking victims.

After lunch, my friends and I rode in the Palmers' SUV to the 20 acres where the Palmers were developing their project. Sandra shared about the future home and the girls who would live there as if the girls were already standing next to her. Sandra's heart was clearly motivated to change the lives of women who had endured the worst of suffering by offering a safe place filled with the love and compassion of Jesus.

This experience moved me so deeply that I ended up joining the board of directors of this small effort to change the world and later began flying between my home and Houston to attend meetings and assist in their efforts. We were confident that by the end of the year, we would be offering assistance to girls to begin the path toward a new life free from trafficking.

Then everything changed. A friend called me Saturday morning on April 24, 2010 to report Sandra had died in a car accident in Harrisburg, Pennsylvania following a speaking engagement for Home of Hope. She and a pastor's wife had been stuck in traffic on the interstate following a speaking event, and a tractor–trailer crushed them from behind. Both women died instantly.

Since Sandra's family was from North Carolina, her funeral was in Greenville rather than Houston. My friend Charles and I took the seven-hour road trip to mourn with family and friends. The minister shared that

Sandra began her efforts to change lives at an early age. As a child, she would line up her dolls on the bed and tell them Jesus loved them. Her message had continued through her entire life, even up to just an hour before her death.

About 25 people had flown in from Texas to attend along with numerous family members from North Carolina. Though a time of great sadness, there was complete agreement about one thing—Sandra's dream to build a home of hope would continue.

At this point, plans are still in the works, but Sandra's Home will soon stand as a beacon of hope to girls in need of a changed life.

Dreams are like that. If the dream is big enough, it can extend far beyond the life of the person who dreamed it. Sandra's dream has inspired thousands, and it will change the lives of many at the deepest level.

There are many takeaways from a story like this—the need to fight modern slavery, the sadness of the death of a friend—but this is the one thing that stands out to me the most from Sandra's story: When God calls you to act, then act. You may not accomplish the entire plan, but you will accomplish God's plan for your life.

Martin Luther King, Jr.'s last speech, given the night before his assassination, shared that he had not yet crossed into the promised land, but he had been to the mountaintop, and his eyes had seen the glory of the Lord. He had witnessed significant social change as the result of his efforts, yet much work remained. He rejoiced in what had taken place, but he was also looking ahead.

What are you doing with your life that will outlive you? What dream has God placed in your heart with such burning passion that you know you were created to do it? What do you want your friends and family to say about your life at your funeral? What legacy will you leave to those who follow in your footsteps?

Just before Sandra's death, I interviewed Christina Mackenzie, another woman whose goal is to change the lives of young women caught up in the atrocity of sex trafficking. Based in the Dallas area, she had already heard about the work of Sandra in Houston and planned to connect with her more to learn how to better serve the needs of sex trafficking victims.

One particular story Christina shared reveals why I admire her so much. She told me about a meeting that introduced her to helping women in the sex industry:

———————

"October of last year, I had a life-changing conversation with the first girl...I had ever met who was involved in the commercial sex industry. Her name is Kami, and I met her through dialing her phone number from an online advertisement. I was very nervous and fearful of rejection when I dialed her number. She answered the phone, and by the Lord's grace, she didn't hang up on me when I told her who I was and that I wanted to meet with her. She then surprised me even more when she said that she would meet me at a public location in Dallas—a local Starbucks.

"When Kami drove up to Starbucks and got out of her car, I immediately knew that it was her. She stood out in her appearance, clothes, and makeup. She claimed to be 19 years old. We talked for a couple of hours, and believe it or not, we laughed and cried together in the process. She had a history of low self-esteem, and she had gotten involved in a bad relationship with her boyfriend, who told her she would exchange sexual services for money in order to help with their finances. Through this conversation, she found out that he was not really her boyfriend...[He was] a pimp, [and she had become involved with him]...

"During our time together, she showed me where her pimp had 'branded' her with a tattoo of his name and other symbols of ownership on her body. These tattoos were a reminder to Kami that she was the property of her pimp. They also let other pimps know Kami was taken. She described her life as one of a slave. She was told daily what she was to do, including what she would wear, where she would go, and what kind of posture and eye contact she was allowed to make around other men.

"I couldn't believe that this young American girl had allowed herself to be put into this horrible situation. I asked Kami if she had ever tried to leave her pimp and her life of prostitution. She answered that she *had* just run away from her pimp, but...it was not easy to leave her situation. Her pimp would physically abuse her, and if she tried to leave, he would also use daily tactics of control. He intended to prevent her from becoming independent.

"Kami and I also talked about God and how much He loves her. I explained that He hated the injustice taking place in Kami's life. We talked about how God wants a relationship with her and that He is crazy about her. She wanted to believe God's truth, but there were so many barriers in her life.

"As our conversation was coming to a close, I gave her a phone number where she could reach me. I told her about several services that I could offer to her to get help, and I prayed for her before we parted. Kami was very grateful, but I knew that it was going to take God's work in her life for that help to be substantial.

"After meeting Kami, I was much more aware of how some girls get involved in the life of exploitation for money. It was sad, but it also gave me the knowledge that I needed to continue reaching out to help Kami and other girls like her, one person at a time."

Sandra had a passion to help girls in need and did it. Christina is doing the same. I'm working to do my part. What about you?

It has been said that a great way to live life is to begin with the end in mind. Once you know where you want to finish, you can work backward from that point toward your dream. If you don't know where to begin, ask God. He hears and responds when His children call to Him. But once you hear from Him, act. Don't put it off. You never know when your time on earth is done.

God is calling you to change the world one life at a time and one small step at a time. Begin today where you are. As the writer James said in the New Testament, do not merely listen to the word, and so deceive yourselves. Do what it says.

To see the change you want to see, be the change you want to see.

Beyond Awareness

*Jesus wasn't happy with religious people who talked a good
game but would not act. Instead, He reserved His harshest
words for Pharisees and Sadducees. You know the punch line—
time to move beyond awareness and act. Here's an example
of how a friend and I are trying to make a difference.*

My friend Charles J. Powell is one of the coolest people I know. Many Christians talk a good game when it comes to living out their faith, but Charles really does it. After several years of working undercover and as a Houston cop, he turned to working for a Christian nonprofit. But he continues to use his spare time to put his abilities into action in a very specialized manner—exposing America's ugliest crimes: human trafficking (also known as slavery).

When he first grew convicted to do something about this contemporary evil, Charles found inspiration in the words of Martin Luther King, Jr., who taught, "He who passively accepts evil is as much involved in it as he who helps perpetrate it. He who accepts evil without protesting against it is really cooperating with it." With similar vigor, Charles began to speak out on the topic at college rallies and church events. When students or congregants began to ask for evidence, he slipped undercover to document forced prostitution and labor.

As I mention elsewhere in this book, along the way, the two of us came together and decided to "go big" in fighting trafficking, and are together now in the process of completing a documentary and related book on America's ugliest crime. However, Charles is always one step ahead of me. In November 2009, a major Christian magazine chose to highlight human trafficking and picked up one of Charles' pieces in the process. I was kindly given permission to share what he wrote again here, in hopes that his research will inspire others not only to provide awareness of trafficking, but to act to stop it. He appropriately calls it "America's Ugliest Crime":

America's Ugliest Crime
By Charles J. Powell

Somewhere in the southeastern United States, a frightened young Asian woman we'll call Linn trembles with fear. Tonight for the first time she finds herself in a dimly lit room smelling of pine-scented disinfectant, stale rice and desperation. Faking a smile, Linn stands in a lineup among other women who are much like her, as a man she has never met selects which of them he will pay for sex. She is praying he will choose one of the other girls.

Linn did not choose to be a prostitute; she was brought to the U.S. by a criminal organization that promised her a job working as a maid for a wealthy American family. Yet upon her arrival in the United States, she was raped, beaten and told she would have to work in a brothel to pay the bill for her travel expenses to America—a bill she will never cease paying. Linn is now a sex slave and the latest victim of worldwide human trafficking.

According to the British National Archives, during the nearly 400 years of the transatlantic colonial slave trade (1519 to 1867), a total of 11 million Africans were captured and trafficked to the Americas. When that figure is compared to statistics from the United Nations and the U.S. Department of Justice (DOJ), which report that 600,000 persons are now trafficked internationally each year, one can readily calculate that during the last two decades worldwide human trafficking totals surpass that of 400 years of colonial slavery by a million.

Twelve million people have been sold into slavery in just 20 years. According to other DOJ statistics, thousands of men, women and children are trafficked into the United States illegally each year and sold as sex slaves to criminal organizations.

Human trafficking was defined in 2000 by the United Nations as "the recruitment, transfer, harboring or receipt of persons, by means of the threat or use of force or other forms of coercion," most often involving sexual exploitation or forced labor. Today the problem is bigger than most Americans could ever imagine, and for the most part, the church peacefully coexists with human trafficking right in its own backyard.

Recently I determined to investigate human trafficking in three major U.S. cities—Orlando, Atlanta, and Las Vegas. I began my strange American "odyssey" in Orlando, and for five days I used the investigative and undercover techniques I learned while working in the War on Drugs and as a police officer.

The results were astounding. By the end of the week, using the Internet, the Yellow Pages, and free local rags, and by driving around the city, I discovered 30 illegal brothels thought to be employing women trafficked illegally into the U.S. for the purposes of forced prostitution. All the brothels were within 15 miles of the church I used as a base of operations during my time in Orlando. Most of these establishments were disguised as somewhat legitimate massage parlors and spas, but to the trained eye they were easily outed as brothels.

To make matters worse, in almost every case in Orlando the business was obviously run by Asian organized crime. How could I be sure? When you walk into a massage parlor or spa where not a single person in the building speaks English, and you repeat the process day after day, hour after hour, there is only one possible explanation: organized crime.

A woman doesn't say, "I want to immigrate to America and become a prostitute" of her own free will. The criminal methods being employed are well established and easily spotted.

My method was to enter the lobby of a suspected brothel posing as a tourist who had never previously visited such an establishment. I then asked questions about the services offered there, took a tour of the facilities, asked to meet all the girls working that day and made general conversation for as long as possible to allow myself time to look for the signs of human trafficking-related prostitution.

I continued making small talk until I thoroughly frustrated the massage parlor madam, who would eventually demand that I go with a girl to her room or leave the building. I always left, but not before I was able to determine with reasonable certainty whether or not to label the business a brothel staffed by illegally trafficked women.

A Nationwide Plague

The next city on my list was Atlanta, hailed for years as the capital of human trafficking in the United States. Experts offer many reasons for Atlanta's earning this dubious distinction. Some cite Hartsfield-Jackson Atlanta International Airport, the nation's busiest, as a factor, while others point to Atlanta's geography: The city is a nexus for multiple interstate highways from every direction.

Using the same methods I employed in Orlando, including the Internet, the telephone, free publications and personal visits to suspected brothels, my results were the same in Georgia as in Florida: I discovered numerous illegal brothels operating rather openly throughout the greater Atlanta metropolitan area. However, the criminal organizations I encountered were much more diverse.

According to U.S. government statistics, the local law enforcement officials of Atlanta and other, similar cities are forced to deal with criminal organizations that have roots in Asia, Europe, the Middle East and Latin America, as well as with domestic U.S. gangs, all actively trafficking in persons of varying ages for the purposes of prostitution, pornography and worse.

A popular television ad says, "What happens in Vegas stays in Vegas," so I made this city the final stop on my fact-finding investigation. The first evening I was there I walked three blocks to the Bellagio hotel and casino, searching for evidence of illegal brothels, prostitution and any possible connection to human trafficking. I had one simple rule for my walk: I would not ask for materials promoting prostitution, but if offered them for free on the sidewalk or at a newsstand, I would accept them.

As I walked, I encountered dozens of individuals handing out full-color, business-card-sized advertisements that featured women of different ages and nationalities offering sex for money. Most of these hawkers appeared to be illegal immigrants working day labor, handing out the cards for some entity not readily identified. In just three blocks, I was handed more than 100 of these cards!

I also found a news rack featuring free publications that offered women for sex who could be sent to a person's hotel room within 20 minutes. But in spite of the fact that prostitutes were readily available, I saw no overt connections to human trafficking.

So I hailed a taxi at the Bellagio, and within 10 minutes the driver had taken me off the Strip to an area of town where he showed me numerous massage parlors and spas that operated as fronts for full-service paid sex. There I discovered many businesses offering women from various countries who spoke little or no English. In Las Vegas, just as in Orlando and Atlanta, I found telltale signs of probable human trafficking in several of the establishments I visited that night.

Big cities are not the only places plagued by human trafficking. In rural Northeast Georgia at least four interstate highway "spas" that offered sex with Asian women opened in recent years, proving that human trafficking is not a problem known only to big cities. (These "spas" were eventually shut down by law enforcement.)

In the final analysis, human trafficking is now everywhere in the United States, whether its victims toil as sexual slaves, industrial sweatshop workers, domestic servants or "agrislaves" [agricultural slaves] on farms. There are victims of modern-day human slavery near the places you live and go to church right here in the United States.

Right now, somewhere not too many miles from where you are reading this article, men, women and children are being forced to do the unthinkable…against their will, against the law and against what God wants for their lives. It remains to be seen what the church will do to combat the enemy in the battle against modern-day slavery. So far, just down the street from your church, he seems to be winning the war—with little opposition from the body of Christ.

Linn is waiting…and time is running out fast.

Such stories certainly disturb us, but often we do nothing to act. Unfortunately, the majority of leaders fighting trafficking in the U.S. at the moment are not led by people who follow Jesus but rather everyday people who want to see this problem stopped. My dream (and that of Charles) is that five years from now, when a person asks, "Who is working to stop human trafficking in our country?" the answer will be that there are thousands of Christians working to prevent trafficking and to care for survivors. If so, mission accomplished. Until then, I'm sounding the alarm to you and your friends to act in this area. If those who claim to follow Jesus can't stand up against the sale of children and women in our own communities, what will it take to move us?

Charles J. Powell is the founder of Mercy Movement, a Georgia-based social justice group dedicated to fighting human trafficking through undercover investigations, the written and spoken word, community education, and when possible, rescuing victims of slavery. You can contact him at mercymovement.com.

Porn Is Not the Problem—
You Are (Dude Chapter)

*Accountability only works if you want it to. Porn exists because
people consume it—lots of it. The problem is ultimately
not just the content. It's inside those who consume it.*

The United States now spends more than $13 billion per year on porn. Oh, and our country also generates approximately 89 percent of the world's pornographic websites. As you read this sentence, 28,000 people are viewing a web page with adult content.

That number exceeds the entire population of the county where I graduated high school. And is higher than the population of the Vatican City, though I doubt there are many (or any) such websites there.

Based on these and other creative statistical arrangements, a person could easily get the idea that porn is one of our nation's greatest evils. One writer has even published a book entitled *Porn Nation*.

As people who claim to follow Jesus, Christians are advised to install filters on their computers or even take a baseball bat to their monitors. The New Testament verse that says, "If your eye causes you to sin, gouge it out" is used as justification for extreme accountability, checklists, conferences, and other such tools to correct this perverse addiction.

But after listening to a ridiculous number of young men share their struggles with the porn monster, I've discovered a truth that is awkward to share but needs to be said.

Porn is not the problem—you are.

Pornographic materials have existed for centuries. Even the cultures of the Old Testament included lewd statues designed for the same end result (masturbation) that today's mobile phone pictures and videos elicit among Western middle-schoolers.

Now you're thinking, "But isn't pornography itself sinful? What about…?" Wait just a minute. Let me be clear: Porn is sin. I can't be much clearer than that. Porn—is—a—sin. But what you do with porn is *your* problem, not the fault of the adult entertainment industry.

Tougher laws and your Internet settings won't solve the real problem. It's another little four-letter word. But it's not in a magazine—it's inside your chest. (The word is *lust*.)

The problem is your heart.

And mine.

I remember the first time I saw a naked woman on television. A friend had cable (I didn't) and I happened to be at his house that day when his mom was outside. I might have been seven. He was nine.

This is all I remember: I was walking out of his bedroom, trying to decide whether I should use the X-wing fighter or the *Millennium Falcon*, and my friend excitedly whispered to me, "Watch *this*!"

He slipped in an unlabeled VHS tape that forever changed my innocence. Naked women unashamedly performed acts on a TV screen for *me* to watch. I was too young to understand why anyone would do such a thing or would even want to watch these lurid images. When his mom began walking up the trailer steps, the image disappeared, the tape ejected, and it conveniently disappeared under the couch.

And I forgot which spaceship I had planned to use for my next battle.

Once a child views pornography, there is no turning back. By God's grace, I was raised in a home where such images only surfaced during slumber parties at a friend's house or when I was trying to choose a candy bar at the convenience store and walked into the wrong aisle. But kids are often introduced to images at an early age on a repeated basis until it is what they think about, dream about, and act upon.

In psychology, I think the technical term is called *brainwashing*.

When a person is conditioned to accept certain images as normal, porn becomes an acceptable part of life. It takes concerted and diligent effort to reverse and alter the process.

For most of us, it takes God.

———

I attended (and graduated from) one of the most prestigious evangelical seminaries in America. During my time there, I led a couple of small groups of guys in what was called *spiritual formation*. These groups were designed to allow students an opportunity to integrate their theology into their personal lives.

We realized that those of us preparing to lead the church were struggling with the same issues as the people we would later serve. One of the common addictions mentioned was pornography.

One Christian ministry performed an anonymous survey of pastors and found that 54 percent of ministers had viewed porn in the last year. My experience has confirmed that this is about right. Not every preacher is struggling with this demon, but enough are that it can no longer be hidden by powering down the computer when a parishioner unexpectedly enters the pastor's office.

The positive of the seminary groups I mentioned were that when we talked openly about the issue of lust (which is the root of pornographic temptation), everyone stopped viewing porn. It was when each individual isolated himself that the temptations would return and addictions retained their former status.

Accountability is great, but it's greatly overrated. It works, but it only works if you want it to. I once met with a student for over a year before he sucked it up and revealed that he regularly masturbated. Once we talked about it, he stopped and only had a few relapses.

People are good at lying, and most of us are good at letting people lie to us. The whole accountability bit is necessary for change, but change will not take place until you decide that you as an individual are ready to do something.

———

One popular Christian psychologist has argued that the *M*-word (masturbation) is not a sinful practice that parents should be worried about regarding their teenage boys. His book has sold over a million copies. It was probably purchased by a million teenage boys as Christmas gifts for their mothers.

One question rocks this whole stupid nonsense: Can you masturbate without *lusting*? I'm not talking about wet dreams or what you do with your spouse. That's different. I'm talking about getting a kick from some image or thought that pushes you beyond self-control into some short-lived, personal ecstasy. It cannot be done. Lust is sin. Stop masturbating.

———

Saint Paul told his young protégé Timothy to treat younger women in the church as sisters. If Christian men could apply this one concept, *Christian porn addiction* would become an oxymoron. If someone were viewing my sister's body in the way that even so-called soft porn does, I would *not* turn the other cheek. I would turn his cheek and maybe even break it. It is unacceptable, and it will not be tolerated.

So guys, next time you are tempted to view porn, consider the woman you are about to look at as your sister. How does that change your world? Enough said.

Porn is not the (ultimate) problem—you are. This is one of those old-school, fire-and-brimstone issues where you need to repent, ask God to forgive you of your ugly sin, and strive to find some help so you'll never do it again.

So quit your whining: "But I'm addicted." "I can't stop." "God says it's okay." "My wife doesn't care." "It's not hurting anyone, so why not?" And all that other junk. Just stop.

Quit sinning and hurting your life, your family, and the reputation of Jesus.

Racism Makes Me Want to Cuss

*My rant against racism in the church, along with my failed
and sometimes successful attempts to do something about it.*

In kindergarten, racism was not part of my vocabulary. My friends had skin of all kinds of colors in our somewhat urban environment. We were brothers and sisters, friends and buddies. Whether learning to tie our shoes or eat glue, we were one family.

Second grade presented a different twist. My parents left the city like an episode of *Beverly Hillbillies*. Only in reverse. We lived in a trailer, used an outhouse for a few months (don't ask!), and we built our own home. We were redneck before redneck was cool.

And I changed schools.

On the first day, I sat in class with twenty other eight-year-olds and noticed something markedly different: Everyone had the same skin color. I distinctly remember whispering to the boy beside me, "Where are all the other kids?" I don't think he understood what I meant.

For the next several years, I experienced the Middle American, all white, small-town world. It was weird. I only saw people of color when we played basketball or football against another school in the next county. And on TV. But I knew people of other colors existed "out there." I silently vowed to find those friends once again someday.

In college, my world changed yet again. This time, I had classmates from all over the planet. Some of them only spoke English well enough to pass the test for admission to the school. I loved it! I took a semester of Spanish, a semester of French, and even half a semester of German. I could say hello in ten different ways and embarrass myself with a hundred new expressions.

Then I moved again, this time south to Texas. Here I learned that racism had only more recently legally ended. Many parents the age of my own parents had lived through legalized segregation.

Though people continued to thrive in a variety of skin tones, I noticed subtle differences. Like the fact that Hispanics worked every position at McDonald's except manager. African-Americans could be my acquaintances but didn't get too close. Asians of various types owned my favorite buffet restaurants or mostly worked at hospitals. Indians had chosen to dominate the hotel business. And Koreans had lots of churches.

I also discovered that real Native Americans actually still existed. They owned the casinos (but only in Oklahoma). And they looked a lot like me.

Later, I consulted some Mormon family research website that pointed out that I too was part Native American. To be exact, I'm one-sixteenth or so Cherokee Native American, give or take a generation or two. Not enough to get the extra financial aid, but enough to grow a ponytail if I want and not call it a midlife crisis.

After grad school, I met an African-American pastor named Dyron. Everyone called him "D"—like the letter—which was sometimes confusing because people sometimes called me "D" too, and we would both look up when people called our names.

But we had way more in common than the first letter of our names.

———

D told me he was born in a little town called Whitewright. From the start, he knew life was stacked against him. He would say, "It's tough to grow up as a black man in a town called White *Right*." At the time, I thought he was joking, but the town of Whitewright, Texas is really on the map of the nation of Texas. (Texas only pretends to be a state. It really is a country. Just ask any Texan.)

One day, D and I were drinking coffee at Starbucks and talking about life. I think D agreed to meet there because it was my turn to pay even though he liked IHOP better.

He said hi to someone he knew who walked by. He seemed to know about every other person who walked through the door. But after this particular church member of his left, D told me something that caught me off guard.

"People gonna be talkin' bout us meetin' together like this."

I asked D what he meant. He explained that even though white and black folks pretend to get along a lot in the South, they really don't handle black and white friendships very well. At least in his experience.

Looking back, I should have taken D's comment more seriously, but I kind of filed it into the back of my head for future reference.

Later, I invited D to speak at my church's youth ministry meeting. The students loved him, and he communicated with excellence.

And I thought I might lose my job.

No one had told me that a black man had never spoken to my youth group or preached at my church since it had been started in the 1970s. I didn't stop to ask, but there were a couple of individuals more than willing to fill me in on the history.

I told D I wanted him to preach to my whole church, but I didn't know if I could arrange it. He understood.

He had the same problem at his church.

———

Martin Luther King, Jr. used to say that Sunday at 11:00 a.m. was the most segregated hour in America. He was right, but sometimes the truth hurts. It's like hitting my thumb with a hammer. I know it's not right to cuss, but I sure feel like it.

My predicament now is that I know the problem but not the solution. Could you do me a favor? I have plenty of bad stories about Christians of different colors not living in harmony. I need more stories of Latinos and Gringos and Filipinos and guys with one-letter names like D who are worshiping together, praying together, and living together as brothers and sisters in Christ.

Once upon a time, I read a quote that said all wars are ultimately civil wars because we are each brothers and sisters, one to another.

So now my brothers and sisters are not just people of other colors—they're people of different nations and civilizations as well.

And I ask myself if I could really love Osama bin Laden. After all, I wanted to kill him after 9/11, but I couldn't get a flight out of the country.

———

When I look beyond my own little world, I have to ask hard questions: Is our interference in the Middle East really saving more lives than it is destroying? Would terrorists really kill my friends if we quit hunting them abroad? I just don't know. I'm glad I don't have to be the one to send troops away from their families at Christmas. But if Palestinians and Wahhabis and radical Shiites and Vladimir Pudding and even his buddy Acmadinnerjacket are supposed to be people Christ died for, shouldn't I at least pray for them?

Maybe I could even have coffee with President Hugo Chávez of Venezuela and have him help me brush up on my Spanish. He might even let me say a word or two about how Jesus could change his heart in a way that changing the oil prices in his favor could never provide.

But commuting to work, listening to Christian radio, honking at people who cut me off with fish symbols on their bumpers, and complaining about racism is easier for me. Actually doing something about racism is not so easy.

Next time I see D, we're going to talk about this racism thing. We're going to do everything we can to help people turn color-blind and border-blind. We'll treat illegal immigrants like sisters. And we'll love terrorists as friends—after all, Christ died for them too, and He wants to change them.

Because that's what Jesus would do.

Here's my confession: I hate racism, but I do little to change the predicament. I hate racism more when it's personal, so I often don't get personally involved. But Jesus forces me to get personal.

With Him.

With others.

With anyone who will let me share His love for their lives. To erase racism, we must become erasers.

Thanks, Dad!

Today marks ten years since my dad passed away at age
49. I told him I loved him, but I never said thanks.

Ten years ago, my father passed away after a long bout with cancer. He
was 49 years old.

When people talk about finding the cure for cancer, many think about
pink ribbons or 5-K runs. I dream about what it would be like if my dad
were still alive. Holding his grandchildren. Telling stories. Sharing life.

The Burroughs family had resided in Spencer County, Indiana since
the early 1800s, settling the county along with relatives of Abraham Lin-
coln's. My dad grew up in a hard-working Indiana family helping his
father, who owned a small-town gas station and repaired cars. By the time
I was born, my dad was a construction worker whose daily return home
frequently brought with it the aroma of concrete dust.

When I hit high school, my parents called my two siblings and me
together for a family meeting and revealed my dad had been diagnosed
with cancer. My brother, sister, and I did not exactly know what that
meant, but we knew it wasn't good. As we would soon discover, cancer
involved daily trips for radiation nearly three hours away in Indianapolis,
as well as the rapid loss of my dad's hair.

I was 15. That's easy for me to remember because I was the only one
available to drive Dad to radiation one day. I only had my learner's per-
mit and had never driven in Indianapolis, but I figured it was the least I
could do to help the cause. The road trip to the cancer center was pleas-
ant enough. But after we arrived, I watched as my dad was hooked up to
a bunch of wires and tubes to begin the radiation treatment process. I distinctly recall closing my eyes just so I wouldn't have to watch it all.

On the trip back, Dad was physically weak and napped most of the three-hour return. There were a few inches of snow on the ground, forcing me to drive with a hyper-awareness of the road ahead. Yet as opportunity allowed, I would glance over at this guy who raised me, praying he would make it to see me graduate from high school or at least until I had my driver's license.

My prayer was answered on this one. Following his treatments, Dad was given a cancer-free clearance a few months later. That fall, he returned to finish college because he would no longer be able to sustain the physical labor of construction for a living. To pay the bills, he also worked nights at our local jail, where he processed inmates and did his homework while watching *Cops* on TV. My mom ended up working more too, leaving my sister, brother, and me to fend for ourselves a lot, but at least we had Dad. Somehow, that made everything else work out.

———

Three years later, I walked to receive my diploma at Perry Central High School in the middle of nowhere, Indiana. While there was much fanfare, all that mattered to me that day was that my dad was alive and in attendance, experiencing the occasion with me. It was a proud moment.

But I didn't know what sacrifice my dad had made to attend. He had been sick recently, but I didn't think that much of it. Shortly following my graduation, a return trip to his doctor confirmed my father's cancer had returned. This time, he needed chemotherapy.

For anyone who has had a loved one endure chemo treatment, I do not need to explain the pain involved in watching someone you care about fade before your eyes. Many recover, but for all, the process is one of the most difficult in life to endure. Many nights, I often wondered whether my dad would be alive when I woke up. I prayed and prayed, and then I prayed again. It wasn't anything complex either. Most of my words were simply "God, save my dad's life!"

God heard my prayer. Once again, my dad became a walking miracle. Three years later (and just one year before me), he graduated from college, becoming the first college graduate in our immediate family. This time, I was the one attending his ceremony, beaming as the proud son and cheering for my father as he walked across the stage to accept his diploma.

———

Life took some crazy turns the next couple of years, including a divorce in our family, my brother and sister graduating from high school and leaving home, me getting married, and a later move to Dallas to attend grad school. My dad then had a heart attack the October after I left Indiana, causing me to return to his bedside once again, wondering if this was my last time to see him in this life.

On the ICU bed where he lay, my dad was hooked to more wires than I knew a person could have in their body. He was weak, but he opened his eyes and smiled when I arrived. He was trying to be strong, but could barely move to squeeze my hand, much less sit up to give me a hug. We both cried for a long time before catching up and talking about his ordeal.

As I left that evening, I said, "I love you" and mentally prepared myself for the worst. Yet he bounced back enough after a few weeks to return home in his weakened state. After radiation, chemo, and years of specialized medications, his heart had taken a beating few can handle. Now on oxygen and a long list of prescription drugs, each day was now a gift to celebrate. In the months to follow, I returned to our old house every chance I could to visit—Thanksgiving, Christmas, Spring Break, and again in May following the end of the school year. On May 19, 2000, I spent what would be my final day with Dad. We shared a burger, took a walk through the yard, passed beside the creek side, and talked about old times.

Without being prompted, my dad also said he was ready for heaven. I downplayed his talk at the time, not willing to consider the void his departure would leave. But he would have nothing of it. He openly shared about many of his failures and regrets throughout his lifetime, but he also noted he had made peace with Jesus along the way. Regardless of his past, he said, he knew his eternity was secure.

Sometimes, it's the little things you notice before a person dies. For me, it was realizing my dad could no longer tie his shoes and that he could no longer stand long enough to cook his own food. I stained the pressed shirt I had worn to visit him while cooking lunch for us, but I didn't make a big deal about it. We shared our drinks, talked about the past, and I shared what was happening in my married life and time in Dallas working with students and attending grad school.

As I left that afternoon, I hugged my dad and told him I loved him, a habit I had kept since the time I could talk as a young child. He said the same and we both teared up a bit. Looking back, I think he knew how close his time was even though I did not.

———

Four days later, a 6:00 a.m. call to my home announced the fateful words—"Your dad has died." His heart had simply stopped beating the night before, passing from this world to the next in his sleep. An hour later, I was jumping into a car to drive the 12 hours from Dallas to Indiana to begin the necessary preparations for his funeral. As the oldest son, I not only had to be there but also had to fulfill my duties to provide some sort of stability in the chaos that would ensue.

I was 23. My mind was not ready to accept a life without a dad, a grandfather for my future children, or a world void of his humor and hospitality. The drive was my chance to reflect, to weep, and to thank God that I had a dad in the first place.

The funeral remains a blur to me to this day. I recall sitting by my mom, reading Psalm 23, and standing in front of my dad's tomb. After everyone had left, my wife was back at the car and I stood staring at the stone with my father's name on it. Below his name were his birth and death dates, July 16, 1950–May 23, 2000. My eyes remained fixed on that dash, that single sliver carved between the dates of my father's earthly existence.

That dash represented every moment of my dad's life. Every meal, every late night talk, every grade of elementary school, the day I drove him to his radiation treatment, and the time we had walked together just days before. His dash was his existence, his contribution, his legacy. He had lived his dash.

———

My dad's friends always said my father looked a lot like the folk singer John Denver. We even had an old 8-track player in our basement with some of his music where my dad played pool with his buddies. One of his favorite songs was "Leaving on a Jet Plane." It was a catchy tune, but the lyrics never made sense to me as a kid.

They don't say much, but music is often like that. It's more about who the song reminds you of and the memories of that person along the way. Now, ten years later, I'm a John Denver fan, just because it reminds me of a dad who gave his love and left far too soon.

Once you start talking about lost loved ones, you often can't stop. Or even know how to stop. Once the door is opened to the memories of the past, the smiles, the tears, and the emotions of someone you cared for deeply flood out faster than you can control.

Looking back a decade later, I realize I told my dad "I love you" many times. I have few regrets about how I ended my time with him. But if I had it to do again, I would have added one more thing—I would have said thank you. Thank you for changing my diapers and waking up in the middle of the night to feed me when I was a baby. Thank you for working hard and long hours at a job you didn't necessarily enjoy to provide for my needs. Thank you for teaching me to throw a baseball and swing a bat. Thank you for taking me fishing. Thank you for teaching me to read. Thank you for loving my mom. Thank you for taking me camping that time when I was five. Thank you for showing up at some of my basketball games even when I sat on the bench almost as much as you did while supporting me. Thank you for dragging me to church when I wanted to stay home and watch cartoons. Thank you for leaving a legacy I can thank you for. Thank you.

———

As much as this story is helpful to me, I don't share it for my own fulfillment. It's easier to suppress the sadness and emotion associated with the loss of someone I love as much as my dad. I share my story because you probably have someone you have lost too. But you're afraid to talk or even think about it because it's too painful. You're afraid to go there because it hurts too much. Let me encourage you: The pain is a necessary part of remembering the joy of the ones you have lost. Yes, your loved family member or friend may have left behind some pain in the process, but most likely, they left some good memories too—memories to be remembered, embraced, and shared.

Remember how much the person you loved showed love to you. Remember how it felt to be held, hugged, or encouraged by your mom, dad, spouse, brother, sister, grandparent, friend, or other loved one. Remember their smile, that one time you shared that you'll never forget.

The road trip. The ice cream after the game. The song that comes to mind when you think of them.

Whatever you do, don't forget. Life is meant to be lived, in all its emotions—not to be forgotten. Continue to share the stories with your friends and children and grandchildren. Let the story continue with you.

I grew up as one of three kids. Now I have three kids myself. I rarely tell them stories of "Grandpa"—it's too emotional for me. But once in a while, I'll bring up the time my dad got me my first bike or the first time I beat him in basketball. Even in these seemingly mundane details, my children come alive as they capture a small glimpse of the grandpa they'll never know. My goal is to tell his story both through my words and my actions. It's the least I can do.

Thanks, Dad!

Divorce Sucks Big Time

*America is, for the most part, a fatherless culture. My
parents have each been married three times. My wife's
parents' history includes a total of four marriages—and we're
Christians. Why are the odds stacked against traditional
marriages? What can we do to become spouses and parents
who follow the path of Jesus regarding holy matrimony?*

As I type, my six-year-old son is sprawled out across the floor of my poorly decorated office watching a Lego Bionicle video on our portable DVD player.

It all started when my wife called and asked me to pick up Ben and Natalie at school because she was home caring for our newborn baby, Audrey. I pulled up to Natalie's preschool in our 1997 Nissan Quest minivan with the crooked headlight and rattling side window and then proceeded to stop at her favorite ice cream store, Brewsters, as we passed the 50 minutes between Natalie's pickup time and Ben's.

One waffle cone bowl of strawberry ice cream later, Natalie and I idled in the parking lot at Grace Academy until our number (143) was read, a walkie-talkie squawked, and my first-grade Lego-lover climbed into his car seat (which children are now apparently required to wear until prom).

Natalie: "Daddy took me to get ice cream!"

Ben: "Aghhhhhhh! I want ice cream too!"

I drove home amid the hysteria. There was no "Hi, I love you, Daddy." I just heard "It's not fair!" all the way to our cracked asphalt driveway (which, fortunately, is only 0.8 miles away).

Ben sulked inside. Natalie squeezed my neck as I kicked the sliding van door shut with my foot and carried her, complete with Greenie (her dirty-green blanket she's clutched since birth), Shuffie (soft, fluffy green blanket number two), My Little Pony backpack, and an array of personal items that each carry their own unique name and story.

Natalie (to my wife): "Daddy took me to get ice cream!"

Ben: "Aghhhhhhh! I want ice cream too!"

Then I said, "Ben, you want to go to work with me?" Tears stopped instantly in place on his cheeks. My little boy returned to life as he saw an opportunity to spend time with Daddy. Hugs, excitement, and adventure together…just with Daddy. Just the two of us.

He never mentioned the ice cream again.

———

As I reflect on the scenario, it points my eyes toward my heavenly Father. Whether He provides ice cream or some other perk is irrelevant. What matters is the time together.

In a word, it's *relationship*. The same relationship we crave with God is the same relationship children desire from their fathers and mothers. Unfortunately, too many stories don't turn out quite like mine. Instead, many of them turn out like this:

First child: "Daddy took me to get ice cream!"

Second child: "Aghhhhhhh! I want ice cream too!"

(Add increasing conflict and escalating drama here.)

Then Daddy and Mommy divorce.

There is no substitute for a mommy and daddy who struggle day in and day out to love their sons and daughters. No federal program, act of Congress, weekend visitation, or pile of money satisfies. A child may own every toy in the universe, but he or she would give them all up in an instant for a mommy and daddy who would be present.

I know this not because of my kids. After ten years of serving among teenagers and college students, I have experienced firsthand that family issues are the "X Factor" behind over 90 percent of the personal problems I have counseled.

College freshman: "I'm struggling with pornography."

Me: "How's your family?"

College freshman: "My parents are considering a divorce. They haven't been in love for years."

At one point, I was an intern at a small church in Dallas that included leading a discussion group for students. In our discussion on relationships, I shared that it was tough for me to trust people in relationships because each of my parents had been married three times, and we were church-attending, divorce-hating Christians. My parents had even led a class on married couples long after they had separated.

On a whim, I asked how many of the ten students had experienced a divorce in their immediate family.

Ten hands raised. Ten for ten.

I think we added up a total of twenty-seven marriages out of our group of ten students, myself included.

———

When I moved to my current home, my family and I started attending a new church. Great people, imperfect, growing, and welcoming from the start. When Mother's Day Sunday hit, I knew we had chosen the right place. A tear-jerking mother-focused video, stories to touch the heart, flowers for my wife, and a high respect that would make any mommy proud.

Then Father's Day came. I was hoping for a similar experience. Instead, the emcee-like elder shared announcements that opened with an *apology* to those in attendance who had suffered with a difficult father. *Okay,* I thought to myself, *I can understand. Now, where's the cool daddy stuff? Maybe I'll win a free barbeque grill instead of a flower.*

No special songs. Zero touchy-feely illustrations. The message wasn't even related to anything regarding fatherhood. By the end of the service, I was at least hoping for a flower.

But it didn't happen.

It's a strange phenomenon in the American church. Mother's Day is a day of honor. Father's Day is a day of shame.

Granted, in a divorce or broken marriage relationship, men are often the instigators. However, the problem is bigger than a guy problem. Or a girl problem. It's a relationship problem.

A problem only the Creator of relationships can repair.

———

During the Christmas holidays, my family usually treks from one relative's house to another just as a rock star does when going on a tour through the country. One night with Papaw and Nanny, one day at Grandpa and Grandma's house, a day with an uncle and aunt, a day at another uncle and aunt's place, and then back home.

During our road trip, my kids have lots of questions: "Why does our aunt have a Chihuahua? Can we have a Chihuahua? Why is Grandma's last name not the same as ours?"

I *want* my kids to ask why their grandparents all have different last names. It's a deeply teachable moment to share the sacredness of marriage and lifelong commitment. Natalie may only care about the big dancing Santa at Grandma's house this year, but as she matures, she'll begin to grasp that our family—crammed with three car seats in a minivan and still loving one another—is quite unique.

In fact, my hope for my children is that they grow up and find families with only one parent a bit odd. Why? Not because the people involved did something wrong, but because they will have experienced a mommy and daddy who pursued a relationship with God, with one another, and with them.

Right now my workload is, to quote the title of a song by the Fray, "Over My Head." Deadlines, projects, and meetings may dominate my job, but love dominates my heart. In Saint Paul's words, the greatest of these is love.

Father's Day currently resembles a day of mourning for many and divorce is as common as office people sneaking peeks at hilarious You-Tube videos while at work. How can we turn the tide the other way? One moment at a time.

Moments when we say, "I'm sorry" after we make mistakes. Moments without words when a gentle hug expresses everything. Moments expressing the words *I love you* instead of just thinking them. Moments where time with those we love takes priority over the next phone call, text message, meeting, deadline, e-mail, instant message, old friend from school, boss, interview, or dollar sign.

Moments. Ultimately, our lives are nothing but a series of moments. Those moments will reflect a soul striving toward a higher calling, or they will reflect a heart pointed inward toward personal gain.

Divorce sucks big time. You can't stop everyone else's divorce. (Believe me, I've tried!) You might not be able to keep your parents together. (Tried that too.) You might believe you can't even consider marriage because it will end up falling apart anyway.

But you can focus on moments. Moments of love that build into lifetimes of love, whether as a friend, lover, parent, or child.

To make a change, you must be the change.

————

I'm about to wrap up and drive Ben home. We'll eat dinner as a family, wind down for the evening, and fall asleep following a few children's books and maybe even a Bible story or two. Something deeply spiritual—like Judges 4, where a woman drives a tent peg through her enemy's skull into the ground to kill him. Or maybe the procedures for offering a bull for a burnt offering and all the blood that gushes out (Ben loves that one!).

Natalie will want to hear how Jesus turned a few loaves of bread and fish into enough food for 4000-plus or laugh at John the Baptizer for eating locusts. (She likes food—just not locusts.) Plus, she has great taste in fashion and has already pointed out that camel hair is itchy and very uncool.

In ten years, Ben won't remember what math homework he had today. He might still quote a few lines from his movie. (Crazy how those lines don't go away.) But he *will* always remember Daddy putting him before work.

And he won't be too upset about the ice cream anymore either.

Pastors Lie About Sex

Pastors like to preach that sex is lame outside of marriage.
Liars! Sex is just as fun. It's the guilt that kills us.

Is sex fun? According to preachers and other abstinence proponents, sex is horrible outside of monogamy. But as well intended as these individuals may be, there is one ugly secret they fail to mention.

Sex is fun whether you're married or not.

Maybe these people do not know this. Perhaps they waited until marriage and do not have any experience outside of holy matrimony.

What will I say to my kids? Will I default to what my parents did and just command, "No sex"? Maybe I'll be more honest with them. Maybe I'll tell them sex is really, really fun, but it's even more fun when you're committed to someone for life and have waited for years until there is only one person you can imagine sharing the experience with.

Unless they're six.

I'm still afraid that when my kids ask me about sex some day, I'll choose the easier sin of lying to make sex sound lame until marriage.

Just like countless parents and preachers before me.

———

It has been said that once you've had sex once, it's really tough to stop. Maybe that's part of why God's plan is for us to wait until we're married. Otherwise, we'd talk about, dream about, and attempt to have sex all the time. (I think that pretty well summarizes much of our culture.)

But there's also a second facet the preachers don't tell you about sex outside of marriage—guilt. The sexual climax is indescribably fascinating. The guilt, however, is depressingly painful.

Many have attempted to replace the guilt with a badge of honor. This is the jock approach: "Guess what (or who) I did last weekend." It's crude, but it is a path many—males, primarily—have walked.

Others attempt to drown the guilt through escapes of various types. Assorted parties, depressing country music, road trips, shopping, Godiva chocolates, video games, pornography, and even church or community service. Each has been used to transfer feelings of guilt from sexual frustrations into something positive.

But people often discover that guilt doesn't go away that easily. It sticks like duct tape to our souls. Peeling it away creates a need to scream and beg for relief.

Maybe waiting for marriage to have sex has more to do with avoiding guilt than we are willing to admit.

———

This year, I had two students in my Bible college class with past criminal records. Of course, these two college guys didn't mention this during introductions on the first day of the semester, but as we got to know each other, I had the opportunity to hear the stories of two men transformed by the power of Christ.

The first guy—I'll call him Jack—dropped out of high school and was caught up in his local drug scene. Over time, he started moving up to selling large amounts of marijuana and other substances, and he connected with top leaders in his regional drug-trafficking scene. After being arrested and serving some time, he spent a few months living with some family members who required him to study for his GED and attend church as part of the exchange.

In the beginning, the church part was just strange. Jack switched from selling drugs and then hanging out with convicts to listening to church people talking about overcoming depression and getting a better job. The experience struck him as superficial and irrelevant. But he kept going. Over time, he began reading Scripture for himself and ran into a few guys who really began to befriend him—regardless of his past.

Jack then had what he calls his Damascus Road experience. Like the apostle Paul, he encountered God, who spoke into his life and called him to change. He called out to Jesus and was transformed. Now, four years later, he's one of my best students, and he's preparing to be a minister.

The second guy—I'll call him Steve—is a quiet personality already working with students at a local church. While serving time for alcohol-related issues and violation of his parole, he spoke on the phone to a guy he had never met about how to know God. It happened to be the right voice at the right time. Steve ended up on his knees and prayed to follow Jesus. To this day, he has never met the person on the other end of that phone call.

Both of these young men are now changing the lives of others in spite of their pasts. How is this possible? There is no addiction-treatment plan, dollar amount, or program that can substitute for the incredible reality of knowing Jesus. A person's encounter with Jesus may not solve every detail in this life, but it does change the heart.

I know because Jesus has changed my heart too. At age 12, I had been raised in church, but the rituals sounded foreign. I attended a church camp that summer so I could be away from home for a week. My cabin counselor, also a musician, performed on the third night of the camp and challenged people to trust in Christ afterward. Many did, but I was still wrestling with how a person could really come alive again and whether this was all just wishful thinking.

After everyone else fell asleep that night, I tossed and turned in my bunk. If Jesus really was God's Son, and if He really did come alive again, I needed to do something about it. But how could I be sure?

Unlike the textbook prayers, I simply remember thinking, *God, I'm going to pray and believe Jesus really did come alive again. I'm not really sure how this works, but I'm ready to try. Forgive me and come into my life.*

I prayed, and something happened. There was no flash of light or audible voice, but one thing changed—I felt forgiveness.

Even at such a young age, I had struggled with this problem that every time I did something wrong, I felt guilt. And it would not leave. Saying sorry or trying some good work to make up for it was never enough.

That's when I first discovered knowing God was not about doing enough right actions to get an audience with Him or to get off the naughty list. It is surrendering to Him, allowing God to take control of my life.

I wish I could say it has been perfect ever since and that I've lived happily ever after. On the contrary, I've had several train wrecks along the way, doubted the path I had chosen at various points, and committed several acts I deeply regret. But through it all, Jesus has been there. He continues to forgive. He loves me just as I am, but He refuses to leave me where I am. He continues to mold and shape my heart. As Mother Teresa said, "I am a little pencil in the hand of a writing God who is sending a love letter to the world."

———

Guilt is an interesting concept. In some Eastern (notably Japanese and Korean) cultures, guilt is a shame-based concept. To say it another way, guilt is more about getting caught than doing what you ought. Guilt results from someone discovering the wrong thing you have done more than the action itself. Shame then results from the collective community and helps prevent the wrong from occurring in the future.

In Western culture, guilt tends to be seen as something we have *done* wrong regardless of whether or not we get caught. The idea is that "I'm guilty" once I do something wrong.

Our postmodern culture increasingly blurs these Eastern and Western perspectives of guilt together. People get to "choose" whether to feel guilty or not based on their own ethics. They only start feeling really bad if they are caught and their wrongdoings are made public. Some have gone so far as to claim that right and wrong themselves are relative. Therefore, they say, we should feel no guilt for our actions.

But the truth is that people who follow Jesus can't decide when they feel like obeying His views on sexuality and when they don't. When a person who is a Christian sins, whether sexually or otherwise, guilt results.

This guilt is often called *conviction*. When a person says he or she is "convicted," they mean that they feel guilty for something they are doing (or are not doing) and feel the need to change. Change, in biblical language, is called *repentance*. So having sex outside of marriage produces guilt. Guilt leads to a desire to change. This has little to do with the sex itself but a lot to do with our souls and how we connect with God.

———

I'm not big on lists, but when I served at a church a few years ago at a place that hated anything with the phrase *purpose-driven* in it, I discovered a list that Rick Warren's church uses regarding purity.

The items on the list are called the "Saddleback Staff Ten Commandments." (Note: The first four do not apply to unmarried staff members, meetings on Match.com, or for leprechauns.)

1. Thou shalt not go to lunch alone with the opposite sex.

2. Thou shalt not have the opposite sex pick you up or drive you places when it is just the two of you.

3. Thou shalt not kiss any attender of the opposite sex or show affection that could be questioned.

4. Thou shalt not visit the opposite sex alone at home.

5. Thou shalt not counsel the opposite sex alone at the office, and thou shalt not counsel the opposite sex more than once without that person's mate. Refer them.

6. Thou shalt not discuss detailed sexual problems with the opposite sex in counseling. Refer them.

7. Thou shalt not discuss your marriage problems with an attender of the opposite sex.

8. Thou shalt be careful in answering e-mails, instant messages, chatrooms, cards or letters from the opposite sex.

9. Thou shalt make your co-worker your protective ally.

10. Thou shalt pray for the integrity of other staff members.

Feel free to apply these to your life as necessary. Why? Because accountability only works when you want it to work, and even then, it only works part of the time. Here's the overarching point of these "Ten Commandments": Don't trust your hormones.

————

A few years back, a pastor named Rob Bell wrote a provocative book entitled *Sex God*. Regardless of one's views about the author or the book, I love the approach this title takes, as mentioned on its back cover. He writes, "God and sex go together. You can't separate the two...because this physical world is intimately linked to deeper spiritual realities. And so, in order to make sense of sexuality, at some point you have to talk about God."

So at least in some ways, sex and God go together. But instead of pastors lying about sex, what approach should we take?

I don't know if I have all of the answers, but I recently spoke with a couple who shared what it was like to wait until marriage before being sexually intimate. What was the difference? Married sex includes no guilt. That is the one essential difference. They do not wake up the next morning feeling dirty. They do not question whether the other person really still loves them or whether they performed to a certain level. It's simply enjoyable.

I used to think not having sex before marriage was a harsh limitation for teenage hormones. Now I realize it is possibly the most freeing principle a person can embrace in following Christ.

Goths, the Amish, Baristas, and Other People Who Like to Wear Black

Wearing black is a symbol of culture—not sin. Love the sinner, hate the sin, and stop complaining that my jeans have holes in them!

I once wrote a book about Wicca, which I discovered is a trendy word for *witchcraft*. I read about Wiccan spells, shared conversations with witches, and learned a few lessons in the process. I now know more about pentacles, lunar holidays, and crystals than many pagans.

As I attempted to share what I had learned with Christians, it struck me that the wall between evangelicals and Wiccans was very high. Most churchgoers couldn't tell the difference between a peace sign and a pentagram. They thought witches worshiped Satan, dressed as Goth-black warriors, wore pointy hats, flew on brooms, drank blood, and wanted to eat their children.

This same misunderstanding extends far beyond Wiccans to other subcultures outside the church. I've been teaching a few courses at a historically fundamentalist Baptist college in my area and continue to learn fascinating (and at times, disturbing) insights into this unique corner of life.

For example, on my first day of teaching, I read from a Bible version called the New Living Translation. You would have thought I had read a text from the Koran. This was big time—a professor quoting from a non-King Jimmy version!

I also discovered that to be a fundamentalist, you couldn't be out after twelve on a weeknight and couldn't wear jeans with holes in them. In fact, hats indoors were taboo, as were PDAs. (I think the acronym was for public displays of affection, but it might refer to mobile devices.) Other no-nos included R-rated movies, Pokémon, McDonald's, thongs (unless they had Bible verses on them), alcohol, Disney (with exceptions for Narnia), long hair for men, CNN, nose rings, and Democrats. In fact, the list was nearly as long as the Gospels themselves.

I discovered the holey-jeans rule the hard way. I wore a pair of such jeans to class one morning, assuming no one would notice or care. That was my first mistake.

My second mistake was walking around campus after my 8:00 a.m. class, allowing veterans of the university to gawk and wonder if I didn't get the memo.

If I had not been a Christian, I might have just cussed. I almost did anyway.

The Jewish leader Samuel once faced a dilemma in which he was told by God to confirm the new king of Israel. He was sent to the home of a guy named Jesse who had several sons. The first son was a jock, an outgoing person, and an obvious leader. When Samuel thought to himself, "This is my guy," God said, "No, he *iz-int*" (New Dillon Translation).

God had a different standard. It was called the heart. We love movies about heart. Whether Rocky, Frodo, or Batman, we crave heroes with an internal passion. So does God. But He searches not just for passion, but a certain type of passion that is focused on Him.

In Samuel's case, none of Jesse's sons passed the test. Jesse's youngest son was still at work with the animals, but when Samuel asked for him, he discovered God's eyesight was clearly body-blind. This runt of a teenager who smelled of sheep poo was Yahweh's choice as the next king of Israel. Samuel followed orders and the rest is history. This stuff is downright biblical.

God looks at the heart.

My wife spent part of her childhood in Central Illinois among another peculiar movement of people in our society who like to wear black—the Amish. These people shun electricity, ride horses better than the Lone Ranger, and can *sprechen Sie Deutsch*. (That's German, for you gringos.)

Every so often we travel to the village of Arthur, Illinois, near her grandmother's farm and sample Amish cheese, check out the furniture, and sip hot apple cider. I love the experience. It's like walking into another country without leaving the country. No passport required.

Once we stopped at a nonelectric general store that sold bulk foods to both Amish and the non-Amish. I was entertaining Ben, my son, in the toy aisle while my wife and daughter shopped for marmalade or butter or gummy worms. I don't remember which.

What I do remember is a young Amish boy in black pants and suspenders who looked about seven. He joined my son and me as we played with the toy farm animals and tractors. We got along great even though we didn't understand each other's culture.

Sometimes I wonder if we could get along with people who dressed in black from other cultures simply by sitting on the floor and playing with toys together.

Not everyone who dresses in black is that different from us. Most mornings I start out talking with people dressed all in black. They're not priests. They're baristas. In case you haven't heard, there are thousands of them out there, each wearing black, smiling, and serving up powerful caffeinated beverages in exchange for your life savings.

Anyway, lately this college-aged lady named Laura has been handing me my drinks. I know her name is Laura because after about 45 cups of coffee, I asked, "What's your name?" and she told me. I think she was telling the truth too, because people usually don't lie at Starbucks. It's bad for their tips.

After cup 47, I discovered she attended a local church that meets in the movie theater where I took my son to see a recent movie. I thought that was an interesting concept. She wears black every day, attends church at the movies, and wakes up each day at 5:00 a.m. She is unafraid to talk about her faith *and* is not afraid to wear black *and* is not a nun. (At least I don't think she is a nun. Maybe I should ask.)

The point is that a person who wears black can be a goth, an Amish person, Darth Vader, a barista, a nun, a Johnny Cash fan, a vampire, a priest, or a player for the Raiders. It's just a color.

So why do we judge people so much by how they look on the outside?

James was the half brother of Jesus. Yes, the Jesus who is God's Son. If you're wondering how that worked, Jesus was born of a virgin named Mary. Mary married a guy named Joseph (but not the same one with the rainbow jacket from Genesis) and (shocker!) Joseph and Mary had additional children. James grew up in the same home as God. Very cool.

James also led the first church in Jerusalem and wrote one of the first books in the New Testament, which was creatively named "The Letter According to James." In it, he discusses that in his day, there were people in church services who would discriminate based on external appearance.

He specifically mentions a situation where a wealthy guy shows up for their worship service and is treated with all the extras and even given a choice seat up front. Later, a shabby-looking, blue-collar guy arrives and is directed to sit on the floor.

James uses this illustration to share a very profound theological truth: Discrimination sucks. Favoritism is sin.

I don't know if the rich guy wore black or not. Maybe the poor guy did. Maybe neither of them did. But discrimination still occurred. And James told Christians to stop it.

I've attended churches that made me feel like I was shopping at the Gap. If I hadn't dressed just right, I would have been the one being mistreated. I've attended other churches where you only really love God if you wear a tie or panty hose. I don't like wearing either of these items, especially at the same time, so I'm usually considered a new believer or a backslider in these churches.

But newer churches sometimes reverse this discrimination. If I did show up looking like a game-show host in a suit and tie, I would be poohpoohed as a fundamentalist in some so-called cutting edge congregations, regardless of whether I listened to Mozart or Moby.

Something's just not right about that. (The favoritism, that is, not Moby.)

If you and I are both following Jesus, would it be okay if I showed up at your church in my flip-flops? That's how Jesus rolled. I hope that would be okay. I promise not to go completely biblical and wear a robe to your church. Unless your church has a Pajama Day. I believe every church should have a Pajama Day.

But on the other side of the spectrum, if I showed up at your multi-sensory church "experience" where you worship God with finger painting and candles, please don't hoard the paints if I show up in khaki pants.

More importantly, I hope Jesus shows up at your church and doesn't find you *or* me discriminating against Him or any of His kids in the audience.

Sin Is Cool. Then You Die.

*Solomon's approach to sin: It's fun for a while, but when the party
is over, then what? (Especially if teleportation doesn't work.)*

Let's be honest—sin is cool. The reason *Cops* and every reality TV show
to follow has had an audience is because people sin. A lot. In very creative ways. In front of a video camera. On national television.

Police car chases are the best. I can't pass up a car chase on TV if I see
it at the Y or in a department store. It's a mix of guilt and fascination all
packed into one little screen. I could start a channel that just showed live
police chases and make a bundle.

Celebrity culture commonly celebrates the good guys doing bad things,
from the infamous O.J. Simpson case to the latest episode of the *Simpsons*.
We also complain about all the bad stuff on the local news at night, but
the station with the coolest footage of bad stuff at 11:00 p.m. is usually the
highest-rated channel in the market.

Sin is cool.

But that's not the whole story. On *Cops*, the sinners get arrested. On
Survivor, they are voted out of the tribe. In real life, we just die.

So sin is cool. Then you die.

That's a problem. An age-old problem. Solomon, called the wisest man
to ever live (following Jesus Christ and maybe Yoda), explored this predicament in a book most of us can't pronounce called Ecclesiastes (That's *uh-
kley-zi-AS-tees* if you're wondering.).

(Side note: I highly recommend reading Ecclesiastes, especially when
you are depressed. You can complete it in less than one hour. If this is too
long, drink Red Bull, and then read the book. It—Ecclesiastes, not Red

Bull—is scientifically proven to be much more effective against depression than country music, according to the latest studies by Scientologists.)

Ecclesiastes is kind of like a Switchfoot CD with a summary at the end. Solomon talks about money, sex, celebrity status, partying, more sex, and a bunch of other fraternity favorites. In the end, he decides they are all meaningless. Why? Because even though sin is fun, we all die. We can die in debt or with people in debt to us (or both), but we all still die.

But then there's always teleportation.

I grew up thinking the idea of traveling through space and time was great. Then I watched Hiro in *Heroes*. Then I was just confused. What do you do when you meet yourself in the future? If I could stop time, why don't I just press pause, party all I want, and then rejoin life until I'm ready to party again?

It sounds like fun, but at some point, there is still that same problem Solomon mentions.

Death.

No one likes to talk about death. Except maybe funeral-home directors, morticians, or horror filmmakers, but that's because they make money from it, so I'm not counting them. The rest of us avoid talking about death for one simple reason:

We're scared of it.

It's the carpet stain in the middle of the room that all the guests see but are polite enough not to mention. What are they supposed to say? "Great stain." It's about the same when we talk about death. "I'm going to die some day. Cool, huh?"

Not cool. That's why, when Christians get fired up or guilted into sharing their faith, the conversation is usually really lame. You're standing in line at Fresh Market next to someone with a loaf of bread, and you give it a shot.

"Nice bread you have there." (You're finding common ground to share your faith.)

"Thanks." (The person is already ranking you at about seven on the weird-o-meter.)

"You know, Jesus is the bread of life." (You are now at level nine.)

"So I've heard." (You consider this an "open door" and cut to the punch line.)

"If you trust in Jesus, you will never need to eat another Happy Meal again. You'll die and go to heaven when you die and are done dying your death." (You now feel proud because at least you were pretty close and got the parts in there about Jesus and death and Happy Meals.)

This is usually the point where the other person pretends she has a cell phone call and starts having a conversation with herself over a phone that's not really on. (Don't ask me how I know this.)

But is there a better way to talk about our faith than talking about death and dying and being dead?

———

My four-year-old daughter Natalie has been learning about Jesus and the cross. Either through my wife, me, or someone at church last Sunday, she observed that Jesus *died* on a cross. When she asked, "Why?" she was told, "So you can go to heaven when you *die*."

That's theologically accurate, but not in Natalie-theology. Last night, she asked Mommy, "When I get down from the cross, will I be able to walk?" *What?* Somehow, she decided that she had to hang on a cross too, just like Jesus, so she could go to heaven. (No wonder she didn't want to go to sleep. I'd be having bad dreams if I believed this too.)

My wife helped straighten this issue out, but it hits an important aspect of true redemption. Jesus came to give us *life*. We don't have to hang on a cross like He did. For Him, it was a sacrifice. For us, it is a gift.

———

Which is why the Gospels focus on the death of Jesus and life for those of us who follow Him. Jesus is the One who said, "I came so they can have real and eternal life, more and better life than they ever dreamed of" (John 10:10 MSG). Or at least this is Eugene Peterson's version of it, which I like very much, by the way.

Good Christians are supposed to have life verses. Verses that they use at the end of letters and e-mails and in their three-point testimony for their classes on evangelism. I picked one when I first started reading the Bible.

Since I was pretty lazy when I started reading Scripture, I chose 1 Peter because it only had five chapters. I thought I was being really spiritual because I almost chose 3 John when I saw that it only had 13 verses.

My life verse was in the first chapter of 1 Peter.

Except the verse didn't have a period at the end of it, so I now had a two-verse life verse. I now thought I was really onto something that would really impress a lost soul listening to my alliterated and nearly illiterate testimony.

Verses eight and nine in the New International Version transformed the way I thought about what it meant to know Jesus: "Though you have not seen him, you love him; and even though you do not see him now, you believe in him and are filled with *an inexpressible and glorious joy*, for you are receiving the goal of your faith, the salvation of your souls."

No talk of death. Just joy.

I understand that we die to self when we follow Jesus, but the eternal life Jesus talks about starts the *moment* we choose to follow Him. We don't have to sweat death so much now. We get to focus on an eternity that rocks starting *today*.

So I've been told reincarnation is now cool too. Buddhists believe in it. Hindus dig it. Wiccans embrace it. Even a few Christians think it sounds all right. Maybe it was in that book called *The Secret* or on Dr. Phil, because I've never read about it in the Bible.

If sin is really cool, then maybe doing it over and over again in different forms might sound appealing to some people. But this strikes me more like an escape from reality.

Everybody dies. Even Jesus died (though only temporarily). Instead of pretending it doesn't hurt, we are called to live as though death is a now-or-then decision. We can die now to sin (not always cool, but necessary) or we can die later and discover why sin is not cool in the afterlife.

Because if the Bible is right about what happens after we stop breathing, there are going to be a lot of unhappy campers in hell. Pastors often leave out the ugly aspects of pain and suffering and just say hell is where people who didn't go to the happy place don't get to sit next to Jesus.

Lots of people also teach that only the really bad sinners who commit sins with an upper case *S* go to hell, like prostitutes and perverts and pirates and parents who yell obscenities at Little League umpires.

Other people have read *90 Minutes in Heaven* or *23 Minutes in Hell* or *5 Minutes in Purgatory* one too many times and think they can pick and choose when they die or where they get to go, as though an afterlife version of SimCity awaits us.

But hell hurts (at least according to the Bible). I'm not as certain about the flames and pointy-horned ringleader parts, but it's clear that the situation is permanent and worse than property taxes and rising oil prices. In fact, it appears extremely painful. And sad.

Sin is cool. Then you die.

But Jesus is cooler. We can die to our self-absorbed lives and accept His gift now instead. Sin will no longer be cool. But we won't have to worry about death so much anymore.

Or whether teleportation works.

Homeless Church

*Church wasn't designed by an architect. (Technically, Jesus
was a carpenter.) So why do we think of churches as
buildings instead of groups of people who love Jesus?*

The church started in a home. Granted, it must have been a sizable home because there were 120 people there, but it was still a home.

Then the church exploded. Not literally (That would be gross!), but it grew really quickly.

Three thousand people joined up in *one day*. But their method continued. Acts reveals that the church met in the Jewish temple courts and in homes. The temple courts were an open area, perhaps the equivalent of an ancient parking lot. When weather permitted, they met outside in a large group. Otherwise, they gathered in homes around tables, engaging in worship, learning, and building relationships.

I like the sound of that. Meet outside when it's nice and in homes the rest of the time.

Sounds similar to the postmodern house church movement or the underground church in China, but it also reminds me of some of my best worship experiences—meeting in small groups around coffee tables, on living room floors, or in classrooms.

During my final year of college, I helped launch a Christian college movement on my campus. We met in Holmstedt Hall 102, one of the larger lecture halls, for our weekly times together. For the rest of the time, we met in dorm rooms, cafeterias, phone booths, restaurants, city parks, cafés, hallways, station wagons, stairwells, and apartments.

When I think back to my deepest memories of connecting with God and other people, megachurch experiences do not come to mind. I've yet to experience God through PowerPoint any better than at a table at Taco Bell with Josh or at Coffee Grounds with a guy named Tim.

There's certainly something to be learned from the early church's de-emphasis on facilities.

———————

Several weeks ago, my wife and I talked with a homeless woman named Rebecca. We had a decent conversation, including some talk about spirituality. She was already connected with a local social worker and had a church home. We ended up encouraging her the best we could, but we felt highly inadequate to provide help beyond the moment.

As I drove home that night, I couldn't help but wonder what it would look like if I had invited Rebecca to my church that next morning. My church is great, but it is a church for suburbanites, not street people. My pastors might argue otherwise, but I rarely meet a homeless person attending our church.

But what if I became the church *to* Rebecca and others like her?

That night, my wife and I *were* church for Rebecca. While I hope she left better than she did before our encounter, she probably still had the same unfulfilled needs the next day, both physically and spiritually. Where are the people who sing "Shout to the Lord" for the five thousandth time when it is time to respond to such needs?

The concept of homeless church is one I continue to explore. If church is people who love Jesus gathered together, isn't church at a café with a few friends just as much church as the 6:00 p.m. Saturday service at one of the "Fastest 100 Growing Churches in America"? Isn't a gathering of thirty Latinos in Reynosa, Mexico just as much church as the gynormous auditoriums built for Sundays in major U.S. metro areas?

I think we would agree the answer is yes. But why do we not live out our answer?

———————

I am currently teaching a graduate-level course called *Ecclesiology*. That's a fancy word for accreditation purposes that means "a class about church." It is designed to cover what the Bible teaches about the New Testament church, along with a little perspective on the college's unique denominational position. Every time I read verses like the end of Acts 2 or the book of 1 Timothy, my heart accelerates for movements and people who really take the challenge to build communities of faith into our world, which has less enthusiasm for church buildings than it may have before.

Humanitarian needs and communicating Jesus' message work best when we don't attempt to separate one from the other. During my first mission experience to Haiti, in 2006, needs exploded in front of my eyes. Poverty, unclean water, environmental damage, lonely children, illiteracy, health issues—and that was just on the way out of the airport.

But who or what can make a dent in such social havoc? Exiting the airport parking lot, our vehicle was flanked by two U.N. military tanks. Yet their presence only kept down violence. It did nothing to change hearts.

About 90 minutes and two gas stations later, I stood atop a little mountain in Gramothe, where I spotted a protruding white steeple. There, in a cinder-block structure, over 500 children receive daily education, food, clothing, and the love of Jesus. It was started by a group of people who call themselves a church.

And they didn't stop there. Medical outreaches assist nearly one thousand people each week when they are open. An orphanage supporting thirteen Haitian boys and girls has been started halfway down the mountain. A training school for church leaders has started to train ministers for neighboring churches. Pastors walk from hours away each week to participate.

Again, started by a church.

When a church, a group of people who love Jesus, lives out its faith, something beautiful happens that guns and governments cannot touch—the human soul. And when the soul is touched, communities are changed, and our world is a different place.

For eternity.

One well-known American church made national news when it purchased a former NBA arena to rebuild into its own facility. The improvements cost over *$100 million*. The average person in the nation of Malawi makes $600 per *year*.

I've grown up in church, worked in churches, and now teach about church, but I have yet to figure out how to *be* church. By God's grace, my journey will lead through future days where I see the name of Jesus honored through the interactions of rich and poor, black and white, Latino and Anglo, Asian and Caucasian, with hands lifted high to the One who created us all—and loves us each the same.

Churches are like friends. They can bring great joy or great sorrow. It depends on which friend and at which moment we look. More accurately, churches *are* friends, connections of people who hold one common bond—the Son of God—whose blood was poured out for the doubters and despised, poor and wise. Jesus communicated these things when He read a portion from the prophet Isaiah:

> The Spirit of the LORD is upon me, for he has anointed me to bring Good News to the poor. He has sent me to proclaim that captives will be released, that the blind will see, that the oppressed will be set free, and that the time of the LORD's favor has come (Luke 4:18-19 NLT).

Good news to the poor, the captives, the blind, and the oppressed. The time of the Lord's favor has come. Jesus has come. He leaves us to be Jesus to those still oppressed and confused.

The church—you, me, and everybody who claims the name of Jesus. So stop complaining about all the hypocrites. Be the church that speaks love, truth, compassion, and grace to those living without purpose and without hope.

Homeless church. Where you and I can both be members because of one homeless man who took our place and gave us grace. Jesus.

Why the Poor Matter
More Than Your New Car

*Why helping the poor is more important than the car you
drive (because smaller car payments allow you to give
more money to those without food and clean water).*

In the developing world, the average worker makes about $2 for a day of
work (that's about how much some writers make typing one sentence).
Seventy-five percent of that $2 is spent on food.

Worldwide, the bottom one billion people live on $1 per day or less.

Let's say at a gas price of $3 per gallon and ten miles per gallon in a nice
car, a person who drives an average of 20,000 miles per year will spend
(wait a minute here…carry the one…add my shoe size times the square
root of infinity and beyond and…)

…a whopping $6000 per year on gas.

That's enough money to buy a used car. (I'll sell you my minivan for
this price. Just shoot me an e-mail, and it's yours!) Or enough dollars to
feed one kid in Honduras for the next nine *years*. By the time the kid's food
money ran out, he could be married and have his own family.

Say it with me, drivers of nice cars: *The poor are more important than
your vehicle.*

I've never owned a new car, and I doubt I ever will. It's not because new
cars are evil. (It's the taxes that are evil.) It's because the only time I cared
about looking cool in a new car was when I was a self-absorbed teenager

lacking the money to buy the sports car or SUV of my dreams. I had no dollars *and* no sense.

Now I still have no dollars, but I do have a little more sense. But I'm finding common sense is not so common among the people I meet. For example, I love good coffee, but last weekend the person in front of me bought one drink that cost like $1900 or something. I think it had extra shots of gold in it.

I exaggerate, but the actual price was nearly $6. They used to call that a value meal at McDonalds. At Taco Bell, it was enough to feed a small village. In some countries, it still is.

Lest you think I only poke fun at other consumers, I admit one of my personal blunders. For weeks, I patiently waited to save a few bucks so I could take my son to see *Clone Wars* at the cheap theater that was only $2.50 per ticket which was a lot better than $9 per ticket. I thought to myself, *I'm such a great dad. I saved a whopping $14!*

Then my son wanted popcorn. And a Sprite.

I again considered how great of a dad I was and thought, *I saved so much money on tickets. Surely I can spare some change to satisfy my only son's deep hunger and thirst.*

We purchased our treasures and walked away before I realized what had happened. I pulled the receipt out of my pocket I had unconsciously tucked away moments ago as we walked to screen eight in time to watch the latest Harry Potter preview.

Nine dollars! I thought to myself in shame. *Nine stinkin' dollars. What is wrong with this world? Popcorn. Harry Potter. Luxury vehicles. The end must be near.*

I could have fed a starving kid for nearly a week!

Instead, I ate popcorn.

It tasted great.

But I felt lousy.

The reason I felt lousy was the same reason you feel lousy when you spend a lot of money on something that holds relatively little value. It's called *compassion*. Some churches call it *stewardship* because they want to tie it together with your monthly donation, but the root issue is compassion. Compassion is simply a desire to help others in need with what you have.

I think we all want to help others in need. So why don't we?

Is it just because we like nice cars and lattes and popcorn? Yes, but that's not the whole story.

At least for people who love Jesus.

People who love Jesus often remember a story known as the Good Samaritan. The usual application is that when we pass someone with a flat tire on Sunday morning on the way to church, it's okay to skip church if we loan the person our cell phone. The other application is that when we see someone in need, it is our responsibility to help. Even if we have something really important to do, we *must* help those in need.

When we don't, we miss out on helping someone God wants to help through us.

It's called compassion.

The only way to change how lousy we feel is not apathy but action.

Because, according to God's Word, faith without action sucks (James 1:22—New Dillon Translation).

The reason those who claim they care about the poor would do well to sell their luxury vehicles is to use more of their resources to help the poor people they claim to care about. A car that climbs mountains is great, but a compassion that leads to action *moves* mountains.

That's why Jesus talked about the poor a lot. And money. And love. And serving others. The four are connected like a good cell phone plan with unlimited minutes and text messaging.

If we care about the poor, we show love with our checkbooks (or online banking transactions). We show love through our vacation days spent in an orphanage instead of getting cancer on a beach. We show love through choosing a job teaching English in China instead of selling gadgets built in China.

If you say you love the poor, great. You're in good company. Such people are called activists. But if you're not willing to make some changes to help the poor, not good. You're in not-so-happy company. They're called *apathists*.

Apathists—yes, I made up this word just now—are people who say they care but really don't care because they don't do anything differently from the apathetic people who don't care and say they don't care.

Except I got to make up a word for them.

I just read an article that claims more food was grown this year than any other year in recorded history. But the same article provided an array of pictures to suggest poverty and hunger continues to ravage nations around the world. If that were my brother in the picture on page 27, I would sell anything I could and send the money to him right now. If the little baby in the picture from page 29 in the top right corner were my baby, I would openly weep.

Then I would do everything within me to change the situation.

But as I type these words with my tear-stained keyboard, I realize these pictures *are* images of my brother. That kid *is* my kid.

And once you and I realize this, the rug is pulled out from under us and we find ourselves facedown crying out to God. There is no turning back once such an insight is made about the poor of our world.

Wouldn't it be worth driving something far less expensive to see poverty changed in our lifetimes?

What would it be worth to you?

Then do it.

Or I might call you an apathist.

Enough complaining. Let me briefly summarize the issue at hand:

1. A new car is generally a waste of money. (Unless you're in the military. Then drive whatever it takes to stay safe and get out of Afghanistan and Iraq as soon as possible.) Application: Sell your fancy car and/or never buy a vehicle that costs more than some houses or requires you to build a larger garage.

2. You can feed entire villages on your NetFlix subscription (or at least a kid or two), so give something to someone somewhere.

3. The poor are people, so shed some tears today.

4. The poor are your brothers, sisters, mothers, fathers, children, and grandchildren. Apply accordingly.

5. Jesus died for you *and* the poor. Equally.

Whatever you do, don't forget number four. Or five.
Because lives are counting on it.
Now.
And maybe even for eternity.

Membership Matters,
but Only to American Express

*Church membership isn't mentioned in the Bible, but
why does the topic make such great sermons?*

Every American church I have ever attended has stressed the importance of church membership. Mostly in the form of sermons or book-
lets, the church's desire to "be connected" usually ends in a commitment
to give a certain percentage of money to the church in exchange for my
name on a piece of paper.

This strange predicament certainly occurs in other countries too. However, in my visits and discussions with church leaders in and from other
distant lands, church membership is rarely mentioned. Rather, the concern of pastors, educators, and missionaries is for the *people* themselves.

I like that. What if I visited a class for guests at a new church and was
told, "We care about *you*. Not your money, what you can do for us, or your
level of influence in the community. We want to see your life changed." I
would definitely appreciate that.

The very fact that American churches have membership classes sep-
arates us from over 90 percent of the congregations in the rest of the
world. Yet churches in the Southern Hemisphere continue to grow at an
astonishing rate while North American clergy bemoan dwindling numbers, concepts such as *dual membership*, and *nonacting* (or even *nonliv-
ing*) members.

My current denomination boasts a membership of over 16 million
members in the U.S. alone. If that's true, about one in every 18 people in

America is Southern Baptist. Something tells me that can't be right. If it is, there are a lot of Baptists cutting me off on the interstate. I can tell by the little fish on their bumper. I think it stands for "Get out of my way. Jesus is on my side."

But lest you feel I criticize Baptists exclusively, note similar trends in other major denominations. For example, United Methodists, the church of my family's background, claimed over 8 million members a few years ago. Maybe they still have me listed since I was baptized in a Methodist church as an infant in 1976.

Roman Catholics do this infant-baptism-counting to tabulate their membership big-time. Do you really think there are 66 million people attending Catholic churches on any given weekend in this country? If so, they should start selling advertising space in their bulletins. Maybe even patches on the priest's shirts like those NASCAR guys do.

If you think I'm the only one thinking this, consider a major study discussed in the book *unChristian* (written by two Christians): It shares that only 16 percent of 16-to 29-year-old non-Christians have a "good impression" of Christianity.*

Half of young churchgoers (people who sit in church services most weekends) said they perceive Christianity to be judgmental, hypocritical, and too political. Not encouraging news if you're trying to increase your church membership.

Membership matters, but only to American Express.

———

Don't get me wrong. Jesus loves the church. He calls it His *bride*. That's probably why He spoke about the church more as a relationship than as an institution. If I had to sign a form to visit my wife, I wouldn't be very happy. If my wife only cared about my attendance and paychecks, it wouldn't make for an enjoyable marriage.

This profound metaphor Scripture uses of the church—calling us the bride of Jesus—could really mess with the heads of church leaders if they thought about it. I once addressed this issue with a pastor. This was his

---

* David Kinnaman and Gabe Lyons, *unChristian* (Grand Rapids, MI: Baker Books, 2007).

first complaint: "Yeah, well, if we did that, how would we get people to give money? I'd have to find another job."

My initial thought was that with an answer like that, maybe he should. Most of the world's pastors are bivocational. Jesus died homeless after growing up as a construction worker. Saint Paul bounced between missionary work and tent-building. As the renowned theologian George W. Bush once said, working multiple jobs is "uniquely American."

If the church is married to Jesus, maybe we should also treat it a little better. I may poke fun at nonsensical religious stuff, but the church is like a queen or prime minister in the Christian faith. Maybe we could quit complaining about how tough it is to show up at 10:00 a.m., and instead we should put on some clothes and worship together with some other people who love Jesus too.

Whether you're a member or not.

People have asked me about my church background, and I'm never quite sure how to respond. I was baby-baptized by a Methodist minister (can't remember his name, though). I also grew up in a variety of Baptist church traditions as a child in a Roman Catholic community, attended an unaffiliated charismatic church in high school, and became "regular" Baptist in college (which has nothing to do with my consumption of fiber). I attended Bible studies by Church of Christ, nondenominational, and even Southern Baptist types. I worked for a Wesleyan church, Bible church, and Assemblies of God nonprofit. Now I go to a Baptist church because they have the coolest children's ministry in town, and I really like going to church in a gym (because at least I can say I went to the gym once this week).

I guess I'm a denominational mutt.

Even worse, I've had to hide the fact that I've worked for some of these denominations to get a job within other denominations. I've discovered this pattern of denominational schizophrenia doesn't look good on a résumé.

I'm not sure if being a denominational mutt helps or hurts in the long run. I've experienced congregations that share communion every gathering as though it's going out of style, and I've been in churches that rarely share the experience. I've participated in gatherings where everyone spoke in tongues, and I even saw people slain in the Spirit. The same pastor put his hand on me, and I almost kicked him between the legs in self-defense. Fortunately, I grabbed the chair in front of me so I wouldn't fall over when he pushed me. I've participated in worship experiences in English, Spanish, Chinese, Creole, and Korean. I've taken sermon notes with more outline letters than the alphabet.

All of these places were called churches of one type or another.

Looking back, I don't agree with all of the practices I was taught, experienced, or even taught myself at times. But for the most part, the churches I encountered pointed me toward Jesus and encouraged me to investigate His teachings for myself.

And I'm glad I did. Jesus loved the church (His wife, if you recall) and gave His life for her. As much as I feel like His wife nags me sometimes, I want to have the same love for her Jesus did. I long to introduce others to this amazing being who changes lives and reflects her husband (Jesus) way better than any other being on this planet.

Whether they ever join my version of church or not.

———

I'll share a little secret: I used to hate church. I still showed up on Sundays, but I hated it. I had worked for a few and had butted heads with the politics and scandals too much to look at it with a Thomas Kinkade-like nostalgia.

Children's ministers hiding porn, pastors cribbing sermon notes from their favorite author, trash-talking about national leaders, and youth workers sleeping with their students. I'd seen it all. I feel like I need to be on Oprah to tell all the behind-the-scenes junk that happens in church that other people in the church don't see.

On the flip side, if the church is the wife of Jesus, I'm learning it should receive a little more respect. I wouldn't tell Oprah or even her friend Dr. Phil about the little things my wife does that annoy me. I love her too much to do that (my wife, not Oprah—at least not in the same way).

Instead of church-bashing, I'm working harder than ever at church-building, but not through membership or construction projects. The church is not a campus but a community. Pastors are not CEOs; they are shepherds. Every time I speak goodwill on behalf of followers of Jesus who gather together, I am speaking well on behalf of the wife of Jesus.

I think Jesus would like that.

Even if you never become a member.

The Day I Dropped Out of School

Education is great, but sometimes a radical change is necessary.
Or as Gandhi noted, "Live simply so that others may simply live."

One day I dropped out of school. And not just any school. I dropped out of my doctoral program at one of the top Christian graduate schools in the country. Why? The answer might take a little explaining.

I had previously received a letter from my friends in Haiti. (For more on the story, see "Helping Haiti" at the end of this book.) They were sharing their plans to add a thousand kids to their school by adding afternoon school. It's the same concept as adding a second service at church. One group of children attends in the morning, and a second group will soon attend in the afternoon. Since the earthquake, Mission of Hope has been left not only with the task of starting back up their own school after three months of disaster relief, but also helping thousands of additional kids whose schools are now rubble or who didn't attend school even before the quake.

Here's a stat that just humbles me: I can send a child to school—lunch and uniform included—for only $30 a month. My doctoral course is currently listed at $615 per credit *hour.* In other words, I can take one three-hour doctoral course, or I can send a child to school for the next five *years.*

The more I think about the math, the more convicting this information becomes. For $100, I can help a mother in Rwanda develop her own business to feed and provide shelter for her family, empowering an entire generation displaced by war and devastated by poverty. I would spend more than that on my textbooks for one course.

According to CharityWater.org, I could cover the expenses to build a freshwater well in a village and provide over 250 people with clean drinking water for the same approximate expense of nine credit hours of doctoral courses ($5000). (Note: Approximately one *billion* people worldwide do not have access to clean water.)

Of course, my missional math has its limitations. Education is critical, but how much is enough? Do I really become more educated simply by adding a couple of letters to my name and a piece of paper to my wall? Will it make a difference to the "least of these" of whom Jesus speaks in His teachings?

God certainly calls some to study as doctors, lawyers, physicists, and other vocations that require a tremendous amount of formal training. But ministers (among others) are often guilty of piling on degrees to make themselves feel better about themselves or to win popularity among peers. Instead, they should be devoted to *true* learning, improving the lives of others. Some pastors are still trying to impress a dad who died years ago with some symbol of success, whether it is with a degree or new church building. Others are still trying to become the cool kid in their high school class, even though they graduated over a decade ago.

Even worse, many see a degree as simply a ticket to more income. While often true, if money is the goal, higher education is becoming an increasingly difficult investment to justify. If a private Christian college charges $20,000 or so a year for four or five years, that's nearly $100,000 to come up with, either now or to be repaid in loans after finishing school. That amount of money could finance an entire village or the full yearly budget of many small NGOs doing great work among the poor around the world.

Again, I'm not being critical of those who attend college, grad school, seminary, culinary school, beauty school, or any other form of education. What I *am* saying is that as I pray about what is more important in life, educating a child with no schooling ranks far higher than another degree for my credentials. I am already blessed with a well-fed family, a home, a job, and plenty of corresponding taxes. My pals in other parts of the world cannot identify with anything but the taxes part.

———

So here's how it went down: I woke up this morning after considering the above and wrote to my contact for my doctoral program:

Dear Doctoral Program Dude,

Just a quick update. At this point, I'm not planning on being able to do my doctoral program any time soon. Please feel free to drop me from your list.

Thanks,
Dillon

I could have given him my math above, but I opted for the short version. Plus, I've got a world to change...

———

But what do you do after you drop out of school? (Grad school, that is. I highly advise against dropping out of high school, and I certainly encourage my daughter to finish preschool.) I guess I'll do what every other dropout does—start a business.

Of course, my business is not about making money, but making a difference. In the past, that usually meant starting a nonprofit so people who made lots of money could give some to people who didn't and help other people who didn't. But that's not what I have in mind. I'm still working; I'm still not to the point where I feel the need to start a 501(c)(3) or other corporation.

Instead of a business, I'm more concerned about launching a movement. Why? There are plenty of businesses and organizations. What this world needs are more people who love Jesus and are ready to move forward to live out what they believe. So this is my plan. If you're ready to do something that changes eternity by changing what you do today, let's connect and try something. You can find me online by typing my name into whatever search engine you use or just send me a good old-fashioned e-mail at dillon@dillonburroughs.org. Tell me what you're feeling led to do and how you think I can help.

We might completely fail. But we definitely can't succeed without giving it a try. I didn't drop out of school for nothing, either, so be assured I'm planning to do some damage (in the good sense) in this world before I've lived my dash (see my "Thanks, Dad!" chapter if this doesn't make sense). The best part is that together we can do more good than we will alone.

Actually, the best part is that we'll make a difference not only here and now, but for eternity. Why? I don't know about you, but when I give my life to help others, they usually ask *me* "Why?" Then I tell them, "I love Jesus. That's why." It has been my experience that when people truly believe I care about them, they'll listen to just about anything I have to say, whether it's my view on politics or my theory about what happened during the finale of *Lost*. If I am faithful to my calling, however, I don't waste my opportunities with trivia and factoids, but I share the reason for the hope that is within me.

There's this pair of verses in 1 Peter 3 used by people who defend Christianity to explain why they are all about debates and information. Nothing wrong with debates, but the context of these verses is about much more than proving ourselves or God are right. See how the full passage reads below:

> Finally, all of you, live in harmony with one another; be sympathetic, love as brothers, be compassionate and humble. Do not repay evil with evil or insult with insult, but with blessing, because to this you were called so that you may inherit a blessing. For, "Whoever would love life and see good days must keep his tongue from evil and his lips from deceitful speech. He must turn from evil and do good; he must seek peace and pursue it. For the eyes of the Lord are on the righteous and his ears are attentive to their prayer, but the face of the Lord is against those who do evil."
>
> Who is going to harm you if you are eager to do good? But even if you should suffer for what is right, you are blessed. "Do not fear what they fear; do not be frightened." But in your hearts set apart Christ as Lord. Always be prepared to give an answer to everyone who asks you to give the reason for the hope that you have. But do this with gentleness and respect, keeping a clear conscience, so that those who speak maliciously against your good behavior in Christ may be ashamed of their slander (1 Peter 3:8-16).

In verse 11, the Latin translation of the Bible called the Vulgate offers an interesting parallel to "he must seek peace and pursue it" (my graduate school training at work!). It reads, "*Inquirat pacem et persequatur eam,*" meaning to investigate or seek peace (*inquirat pacem*) and to pursue it (*persequatur eam*). Rather than primarily emphasizing an intellectual pursuit to faith, we find that we are to seek and pursue peace. This theme, quoted by Peter from Psalm 34, is found again in the Sermon on the Mount by Jesus. In Matthew 5:9, we are told that "God blesses those who work for peace." Why? "For they will be called the children of God" (NLT).

Those called God's children are the same ones called to share the hope we have within us, both in our conversations and through our lives. Some would go so far as to quote Saint Francis of Assisi: "Preach the gospel always. If necessary, use words." But that's *not* necessary. We have a powerful, radical message of love that is to be both lived and spoken. The problem is when we do one without the other. It's like trying to walk with one leg. It can be done and with some help, but it's not ideal. You'll never get as far as if you have a healthy set of two legs. The same can be said of our calling to "make disciples of all the nations" as Jesus commands. We'll always extend our reach if we combine both actions of love with the teachings of Jesus.

And speaking of Jesus, there is one complex theological concept I learned in grad school worth the entire 120 credit hours of lectures and coursework: Theologians call it the *Incarnation*. Most of us call it *God with us*. We sing about it at Christmas—"O Come, O Come, Emmanuel"—but often fail to realize the significance of this event.

Jesus, God in human form, willingly chose to leave the comforts of eternity in heaven. He was born to a teenage peasant girl in a small town in a place designed for animals. Jesus grew up in insignificance. He likely experienced hunger as a child and the frustrations of walking to the local well to gather water. Jesus was often looked down upon by those around Him. As He began His life mission as an adult, many misunderstood His work. His family thought Jesus had lost His mind. His followers were confused about many of His key teachings. Religious and political leaders mocked His simplicity. The poor were His best audience, realizing Jesus offered hope, healing, and help they lacked. Ultimately, Jesus gave His life up voluntarily to those who despised Him. It was not until Jesus conquered death through His physical return to life that His followers "got it"—this was God. In a body.

Jesus left soon afterward, leaving His followers with a message to change the world by living out and sharing His teachings with others. It had nothing to do with textbooks or student loans. It had everything to do with prayer and action.

This incarnation, though unique to Jesus, is a model for us today. As with Jesus, we are called to go where others need to experience His love and message, whether on a school campus, in an office, a neighborhood, a homeless shelter, a hospital, a prison, or in lands far beyond where you call home.

I recently talked to a lady who had spent some time serving at an organization in India called Freeset.* According to a story on their website, a family from New Zealand moved to Kolkata (Calcutta) to work and live among the poor. Their location is the red light district of Sonagachi, the largest, most infamous sex district in Kolkata (which interestingly, has no red lights). Within a few square miles, more than 10,000 women "stand in line" selling their bodies to thousands of men who visit daily. Many are trafficked from Bangladesh, Nepal, and rural India. For others, poverty has left them without options. The cries of their hungry children drive them to sell their bodies.

My friend visited to volunteer and learn more about their work to develop Free Trade opportunities for these ladies. There, she learned the story of Shyamali (named changed). The years Shyamali spent married as a young girl were filled with agony and shame. Shyamali was barren. She found little understanding from her parents, who also blamed her for the barrenness and divorce.

Forced from her home, Shyamali went to live with an aunt. There, while sitting at a local tea shop, she was introduced to a man who asked where her husband was. She poured out her story to the stranger. He listened, and appeared to understand. When he offered to take her to Kolkata and find her a good job, she thought that someone finally cared enough help.

Telling her aunt she was going to see her mother, Shyamali left for Kolkata. As soon as she arrived, the man took her to Sonagachi and sold her to a madam. On the first day, she was treated very nicely. On the second day, she was given a very short skirt. She asked what to do with it. "Don't you know where you are?" her madam replied. "Wear this and go on the road and wait for customers." Shyamali refused. Her madam said, "Okay, you pay me my money back. If you don't, all the pimps will beat you up." It was then she discovered that the man who brought her to Kolkata was a pimp.

---

* This story is from Freeset's website at http://freesetglobal.com/who-we-are/our-story. Shyamali's story can be found at http://freesetglobal.com/who-we-are/meet-the-women.html.

Afraid, she put on the skirt. They cut her hair and forced her onto the road. Her madam, still unhappy with her response, beat her so badly that the scars on her head remain today. Sick of her outbursts on the street, Shyamali's madam sent her to her daughter's brothel. There, she and many others were kept indoors, with the customers brought to the women's rooms. None of the women were allowed out of their rooms at all. They never saw the same man twice, just in case a customer took a liking to a woman and tried to release her.

A year later, while the brothel-keeper was in the hospital, one of the women told Shyamali to run away while she could. Shyamali stole four saris, a box of money, and caught a bus to return to her aunt's. Once there, she learned that her mother was worried sick about her. It was hard to go back home, but Shyamali missed her mother, too. She found her mother in a bad state, with a broken wrist. Using the stolen money, Shyamali paid for her mother's treatment and nursed her.

Having few options, Shyamali went to work at a brothel in Asansol for a few months, where she met a woman who took her back to Sonagachi. Her new madam treated her well, and even when she moved to an area close by would visit and check that she was okay.

Five years ago, Shyamali met a man who has become her husband. She has new hope for the future. Today she doesn't have to stand in line and wait for men to use her. She has a stake in a business in Kolkata. Although she has only recently learned to sew jute bags, her progress is rapid. Soon she might become a supervisor and perhaps one day she will count other women who she is helping as her children—the ones she never had.

Shyamali's story is one of millions of people in need of the love of Jesus from ordinary people like you and me. Her life was changed by one family who gave her a job, a way out, and a way up.

When you and I see the needs around us, it wakes us up from our Fantasy Football draft picks and the next *Twilight* novel so we can live with a greater sense of purpose. Then we can live with confidence...whether we are called to drop out of school or go back to school, or whether we are called to help the person at the next stoplight or in the next nation. Only then will our education be truly complete, as we live our lives in a manner worthy of our calling. As the apostle Paul wrote, "Whatever happens, conduct yourselves in a manner worthy of the gospel of Christ" (Philippians 1:27). Whether it takes another degree or not.

If Jesus Had a Blog

What would Jesus say if He blogged today? Or would He blog at all? After all, blogs seem pretty random at times. And Jesus is anything but random.

Sometimes I wonder what Jesus would have done if He was living in today's tech-driven culture. Would He have an iPhone? Would He have a Twitter account, and if so, would He tweet the Beatitudes? Would He text and drive? (I'm not recommending this, but Jesus *does* have superhuman powers!)

I'm not sure if Jesus would have been a *Lost* fan, but He did come to seek and save the lost. I question whether He would be a Mac or PC guy because He was technically homeless during His spiritual tour time period, but there is one tech venue I'm guessing Jesus would embrace.

After much contemplation, one media choice I am certain Jesus would make is having a blog. If anyone should have a blog, it should be Jesus, right? But the problem with Jesus having a blog—as it would be with anyone having a blog—is that people like to sound off their own opinion, ranging from smiley faces to venom.

While considering the theoretical content my Savior—the God of all creation—would state on said blog, my buddy Brant posted an insightful little piece of literature on his own blog, fittingly entitled Brant's Blog of Awesomeness (to read his entries, see MorningswithBrant.com).

Since I believe he truly captured the heart of what Jesus would blog, I sent my DJ friend an e-mail to tell him how much I enjoyed his piece and its life-changing potential for impact. During this said e-mail correspondence, I kindly suggested that Brant should allow me to share his unparalleled literary skills with the audience reading this book, and he generously agreed. He even included a reference to my all-time favorite Way FM song "Last Train to Awesome Town." (Really, if you've never enjoyed the experience of listening to "Last Train to Awesome Town," please place your bookmark here, run—don't walk—to the nearest computer, google the song title, click, and enjoy.)

Good. Now that you're back, I share with you the amazing, one and only blog post contribution in *Undefending Christianity*, from Brant Hansen.

If Jesus Had a Blog

We FINALLY got an internet café in Galilee. The ESSENES have DSL, and we're just getting dial-up. That should tell you something!

Anyway, I was hanging out with some religious leaders. They got on my case for not keeping their Favorite Rules (apparently, you HAVE to wash up before dinner, in accordance with scripture). I told them religious leaders love to have rules to make everyone else feel inadequate.

Oh yeah, they "tithe" and stuff, but my Father is all about people having hearts for mercy and justice, not hearts for a tithing rule.

Didn't fly very well. :0

Posted 12:36 p.m. in Category "Stuff I Was Talking About in Aramaic Today but Now I'm Typing in English"

12 Comments

Comments

Jesus, Love Ya, But I think you're throwing the baby out with the bathwater again here. There's nothing wrong with tithing. There's a lot of scriptural precedent for it.

I "get" where you're coming from a lot of the time, but this is a little too simplistic. I encourage you to continue to learn and study.

—karifish777

I normally don't comment, but I had to come out of lurking here.

"karifish" is right, Jesus. It's easy to criticize and critique, but how exactly do we measure "mercy" and "justice"?

Maybe pray about this and talk to your pastor about it. Oh—I forgot—
you don't HAVE a pastor! (I still remember that "brood of vipers" entry...)

—chapterboy21

J—I usually love your blog, and I appreciate the need for "love" here,
but you're basically saying (am I clear on this?) that it doesn't matter if I
give money or not?

You go off on these guys, but they're following their convictions. I appreciate your emphasis on having a heart for mercy, but that's not the only
issue. We need people to DO things that show their hearts, and tithing
is part of that. I'm glad I tithe.

My dad is a pastor, and I showed him your blog. He said (no offense)
you've probably got a thing with authority. Anyway, I don't think you do,
but you tend to oversimplify things.

—buckeyesgo02

Dude, what are you smoking?

Honestly, I love some of the funny stuff you post here (that cartoon of
Herod was over-the-top, though) but I'm sorry—this is just wrong. You are
too reactionary against religious authority. God put those authorities in
your life. Look it up in the Bible, the Word of God. (I know, I know, I caught
your post about how YOU are the word. Didn't care for that, either.)

—quiettimephil

Oh wow. I *love* this.

THANK YOU for posting this. I have felt like a loser for so long, like I can't
keep up with all the rules and everything my church is asking me to do,
and I feel like a failure as a single mom. And you're saying you just want
to see me love people!

I'm crying. Thank you.

—karen83

J-Train: Love the blog. Keep it comin', brother!

You do seem to lump all religious leaders together. I appreciate your point, but the fact is, there are lots of great religious leaders out there. You've got a little 'tude going on there, and you speak in big, blanket statements.

Yes, our religious system is messed up. But we don't need to trash it. We need to reform it. Blasting our leaders doesn't help. We NEED great religious leaders. I just wish you'd acknowledge that.

Anyway, just a thought from a brother.

—agape4U

Get great deals on meds NOW! Viagra, Cialis online at 50% less at onlinemeds.net! SAVE TODAY ON FAVORITE MEDS SAVE TODAY ON FAVORITE MEDS SAVE TODAY ON FAVORITE MEDS SAVE TODAY ON FAVORITE MEDS SAVE TODAY ON FAVORITE MEDS SAVE TODAY ON FAVORITE MEDS

—yourmedsnow2323434

I linked to your blog from your woodworking site. I had ordered a new wood pulpit, but I'm going to cancel now that I can see where your head is with regard to religious leaders and our system.

To be honest, I'm surprised you have a public platform in Christian ministry and that you're still allowed to do it. I wonder if your audiences knew what you really thought. Would you still have a job?

—preachtheword9021

Yeah, let's all stop tithing. Let's stop obeying all the rules. There won't be any pastors, and we won't be able to pay the bills for our churches. Nice.

While I'm at it, I'll quit as worship pastor and give all my money to the poor. Why don't you quit ripping on everything and tell us how church government is SUPPOSED to work? You never detail that—you just rip, rip, rip.

—onfireforJesus777

Dude...This story is classic.

This is why I try to link everyone to your blog. In fact, my church-planting site is all about trying to get people to believe what you're saying. You rule, man.

I'm so totally with you on the establishment too. Here's the weird thing: Almost as soon as I get a new group of Jesus-blog followers going and try to recognize the mature servants among them, they all start ranking themselves and jostling for position and attention. *Unbelievable.*

I write letters to them, telling them to quit putting rules on people, and then they make rules out of my letters. *Hellooooo?*

Anyway, I used to be one of those guys putting rules on people, trying to make things complex. Sweet gig, that. Thanks—seriously—for putting me out of THAT job.

—saul_call_me_paul23

Love the blog. I think you way oversimplify, and I don't think you're right on all this stuff. But if you are, I just wasted three years in seminary.

—lutherules99192

---

i don't understand the tithe thing but i like your blog and i read the thing about how kids rule and i liked that a lot

i like the little yellow flowers U made UR AWSOME

—horsegirl1999

My favorite part of Brant's blog is the fact that as a Christian DJ who takes on real issues, he deals with this kind of stuff all the time. The first caller (or blogger) is all for his view, the next is the polar opposite, and the third one isn't even on the topic. While we tend to think of radio people dealing with such craziness, the truth is that this is life.

If I stand in line at my local Starbucks, I love to listen to what people talk about or do. One lady might be talking full-speed on her cell phone while ordering a latte and holding her kid, and at the same time, the next guy is checking out how to save ten cents on the menu. And the third person is a high schooler trying to look cool by ordering the right drink and still making it to class on time. Baristas have to deal with it all—with smiles and excellent customer service. I don't know how they would make it through a morning rush without drinking the coffee themselves.

But the same is true if you're a parent, teacher, student, counselor, mechanic, flight attendant, coach, salesperson, politician, firefighter, or grandparent. Every interaction—on its own—appears as chaos with no rhyme or reason.

Without God.

Without God, life *does* seem like chaos. (Okay, in all honesty, it sometimes feels like chaos with God too.) If there were no God, Solomon's pattern of "live and be merry" sounds about right.

But *with* God, it's a different story. That's why if Jesus had a blog, He could hear every opinionated voice out there and make sense of it. Why? He is not only the Word (John 1:1), He is also love (1 John 4:8).

As God's children, God's love enters our hearts and the apparent randomness of daily life has meaning. We still don't always know what some things mean or why bad things happen to good people, but we know there is a purpose (a destiny) to our lives.

And if Jesus had a blog, He would talk about purpose—a lot. Not just in the *Purpose-Driven Life* sense that lasts 40 days, but in the "change your life forever" sense.

But if this is not making sense, let me share an example. Six years ago, I was working at a conference in Denver for a company that did technology for churches. When we returned to Indianapolis, the convention center shipped back our exhibitor materials—along with one random plasma-screen television.

We called around and discovered it belonged to this group called Convoy of Hope. They deliver disaster relief supplies. Why they had a plasma TV, I have no idea. But they were in Springfield, Missouri, which left the problem of getting their oversized screen back to their office from ours.

That weekend, I also happened to be talking with my wife about the car her sister, Marla, was giving to their parents. Since her parents lived in Indiana, they needed a way to get it from Dallas, Texas, where Marla lived, to their home. In passing, I suggested I could go down with my wife's brother and get it, meeting somewhere in the middle. I was suddenly set up for a Saturday road trip.

The next day, I told my boss I was headed to Missouri that weekend and wondered how far away Springfield was from our road trip itinerary. On a map, Springfield was almost exactly in the middle of our journey. My road trip was now a road trip and delivery trip. The big TV was headed out with us to Springfield.

Saturday came, and my brother-in-law and I took off in his car from Indianapolis to Springfield with a big television, loud music, and plans to come back with another car for his parents. Six hours later, we were in the parking lot of Convoy of Hope, and we dropped off "the package."

My wife's sister and her husband were driving up in two cars to drop one off to us, and they were about 45 minutes behind us in time. This left us some time to sit in a parking lot and talk about life. We talked about a lot of stuff—we were both in transitioning periods at that time—and had some great conversation about what God would have for us to do. My traveling partner talked about his career and relationships, and I told him about my desire to write and possibly do something mission-related in the future.

Soon our relatives arrived. We chatted for a bit, picked up the keys, and drove the second leg of our road trip back to Indiana. It was a good day. Random, it seemed, but good.

Six years later, Doug is happily married, successful in his job, and I'm writing. But that's not the whole story. The Haiti trip I discuss at the end of the book was about five years after that Saturday road trip. My first night in Haiti, I was talking with this guy who had been distributing food all day in a tractor-trailer.

I asked him who he was there serving with. "Convoy of Hope." My brain did that fast rewind thing that happens when someone mentions a name you know from somewhere. A moment later, I replied, "Convoy of Hope? You mean the place in Springfield?"

"You *know* about us?"

"Kind of," I answered, "It's kind of a long story."

All that to say, there is no *real* randomness in life. God used a little road trip years ago to remind me that in the middle of some crazy transition, He was preparing me to serve alongside people years in the future who would work at the same place as the organization where I was running errands and praying about life.

You probably have some of those stories too. Maybe you need to take a few minutes to stop and think about them. Maybe you should even blog about it.

Go and do likewise.

"I Caught You a Delicious Bass"

*Words that could apply to both Napoleon Dynamite and
Jesus (see the last chapter of John's Gospel). Why giving rather
than asking is the first step in building relationships (and
how the church screws this up all the time). Heck yes!*

My confession in this chapter is simple: I like *Napoleon Dynamite*. Next
to *Star Wars*, it may be the greatest film ever created. I've rented it,
downloaded it, purchased it, pondered it, quoted it, and spread its glory
far and wide.

Ligers rock (and I have the T-shirt to prove it).

One of my favorite lines is at the very end of the film. Napoleon wants
to make things right with Deb and says, "I caught you a delicious bass."

He then follows up with, "You wanna play me?" Deb nods and they
end the film playing tetherball together, united once again.

Near the end of the Gospels, we find a similar story (minus the tetherball). Jesus is alive again, but His friends haven't seen Him recently and
decide to take a fishing trip. Who knows if they shared liger stories or
played Texas Hold 'Em on the boat, but they caught nothing that night.

As the sun began to rise, they spotted a guy on the shore. The guy suggested they throw their net on the other side of the boat and see what happens.

I don't know about you, but on those really fancy fishing shows on TV,
it doesn't really matter too much which side of the boat the net is on. The
fish don't see the net on the other side and say, "Hey, guys, look! The net
moved. Let's jump in!"

But in John's story, that's what the fish did. There were suddenly so
many fish that seven grown men couldn't pull in the catch.

The clue phone was ringing, and Peter was the first to answer.

He shouted, "It's the Master!"

As the impulsive leader of the bunch, Peter abandons ship, fish, chips, and friends to dive into the water and swim toward the shore. I'm not sure if he was hoping to use his superpowers to walk on the water again and they didn't work or not. Either way, I guess he wasn't very hungry anymore. He just wanted to be close to Jesus.

His other six buddies finally hauled in the catch and noticed that Jesus had already roasted some fish over an open fire along with some bread. In Napoleon's words, "I caught you a delicious bass."

They ate. But the credits didn't roll up the screen just yet.

––––––––––

There is then a confusing conversation where Jesus asks Peter if he really loves Him. Each time Peter says he does, Jesus tells him to feed sheep or lambs or raptors. In English, it makes little sense. But in the original language, there are two different words tossed around for love.

Jesus asks if Peter *agape*-loves Him—that is, whether he loves Him with the deepest, truest love. Peter answers with, "I love you like a brother," using a different word for love. This happens twice.

The third time, Jesus flips the question. "Peter, do you love me like a brother?" That was a kick to the groin. Peter attempted modesty because he had denied Jesus three times when he had been arrested. He didn't feel like he could claim to love Jesus with a loyal love.

Peter responded, "You know I love you like a brother. You know everything."

Jesus then challenged Peter's loyalty with two words that transformed this burly fisherman forever: "Follow Me."

Peter did. He led the first 120 Christians. He spoke out on the Pentecost holiday to lead 3000 newcomers to join this new Jesus movement. He traveled throughout the Roman Empire to share the perfect love Jesus offers.

Then Peter died for following Jesus.

Like his Leader, Peter gave his life for the One he loved.

That's a fish tale worth telling.

––––––––––

In relationships, whether with friends or lovers, we often speak of a give-and-take. This mutual love means we do things to show love to the other person, and they love us by doing certain things for us. This is the love Peter spoke of in his conversation with Jesus.

This works short-term. But this arrangement is the kind of love that alienates roommates, splits best friends, and destroys marriages. Why? Because it's a love based on bartering, not on Jesus.

Bartering is based on *exchange*. Like Craigslist, we trade a fishing boat for a motorcycle.

I barter at a local bookstore, where I trade in old books for other old books. It's great! I buy half as many books and always have new stuff to read.

But what would happen if they quit taking my books? Then I'd move on and look for someplace else that would do business with me. That's fine for books, but not for people.

People need Christ's love, not Craigslist love.

I also call this concept Barnes-and-Noble love.

In fact, I call Barnes and Noble my other church because I go there to be alone with God. And magazines. And scones. And free books.

Lots of free books.

I've read more books *in* Barnes and Noble than I could ever afford to buy *at* Barnes and Noble. I call it good stewardship.

One time I read *A Walk to Remember* by Nicholas Sparks while sitting in a Barnes and Noble in Dallas by Northpark Mall. I was really wrapped up in the story and realized I was starting to openly weep over this teenage girl who was about to die and the guy who loved her anyway.

Then I remembered I was in Barnes and Noble and not at home on my living room sofa!

I read the final chapters with one hand over my eyes in an awkward salute to a book that had softened my heart.

I tell this not to reveal that I occasionally read a Nicholas Sparks book, but because of the environment I find at Barnes and Noble. I can walk in, pick up any book, order a mocha, plop into a recliner, and find rest.

I can't do this at my church. I'm usually late and have to get a name tag for my kids and grab a bulletin and find a seat and stand and sit and stand and bow my head and sit and then stand again and then stare at one person who talks for 40 minutes and pretend I'm taking notes and then stand and sing and bow and shake someone's hand and pick up my kids and find my car and fight my way out of the parking lot (in good Christian love) and pick a place to have lunch and get there before the Methodists do and choose my food and leave a good tip because the other Baptists won't and not get food on my nice clothes and then drive home. It's exhausting!

That's why I have another church called Barnes and Noble.

I rest and connect with God there. I pray and journal and read Scripture and reflect on the problems impacting my community and world. I think about ways I can better love my wife and kids and improve how I work.

I sometimes even talk about spiritual stuff with other people who are there and try to help point them toward the row with the Bibles that is just past the astrology books around the corner from all the vampire novels.

Barnes and Noble will accept me as I am whether I buy a book or not. I'm even a member there. And I'm not offended when they offer me a coupon.

They take me just as I am—without one fee.

———

Christians screw this up all the time. I visit a church, and I'm asked to sign a card, stop by a special room, or take a class. Why? This seems to communicate that if I commit to doing something for them, they'll do something for me.

I sign up, give, serve, attend, and tell my friends to come next Sunday after they shave and put on "church clothes." In exchange, I get to listen to a band, hear a message, and get free child care from ten until noon every Sunday. (I exaggerate, but you get the idea.)

The problem with this strategy is the same problem with prenuptial agreements. You do, *then* I'll say, "I do."

But the church is called to show Christ's love, a love that is upside down and diagonal from the typical approach. If Jesus were the pastor at my church, a new person would show up and get a hug, maybe a sticker or balloons for the kids, and a free cup of coffee or juice to drink during the service.

That's not consumerism. It's called hospitality.

Once I attended and loved how I was treated at this imaginary church led by Pastor Jesus, I would tell some people how great it was and come back again. And again. After a while, I would realize I wanted to be part of this group, no matter what steps or classes or baseball diamonds I had to circle.

I would love this group of people because they first loved me.

That just seems biblical. We love because He (Jesus) first loved us.

What is true for Christ also works at church.

I used to attend a church that had a big fishing trip every year that cost hundreds of dollars and required nearly a week to get there, sit in a boat with a pole in the water, and return. "Wasteful consumers," I murmured in righteous indignation at the poster hanging above the urinal as I conducted my business. But that's because I am terrible at fishing and couldn't get the week off from work. I secretly really wanted to go.

But fishing has a lot to teach us about life. And about love. In fact, I might join the next fishing trip just so I can sit with a line in the water and think about what love really is.

Like catching a delicious bass. And sharing it with a friend. Even if that friend is not always loyal to me.

Like Peter.

And like Jesus (the bass part, not the disloyal part).

Heck yes!

Death by Potlucks and Krispy Kremes

Gluttony is the most neglected sin in the American church. If our bodies are the temple of God, then American Christians are the megachurch.

All fifty of America's states include a population of at least 55 percent that is obese or overweight. Some states are pushing 70 percent.

In fact, obesity is so common that we have given it new names. Horizontally challenged. Plus sizes. Big and tall stores.

Why?

Because Americans are addicted to food.

Churches are no exception. I grew up in a small church that held a monthly lunch after its Sunday service with more food than the Asian Buffet across the street from my office. When I think of a feast, my memories still rewind back to my childhood days at the pitch-in dinner.

They were more like shovel-in dinners.

Today's cutting-edge congregations are no better. They have simply traded in the pitch-in dinner for the drive-thru breakfast. Krispy Kreme could stay in business in my town solely based on church-direct sales.

Coffee bars are now common in today's mega- and micro-churches, adding an energy boost to worship time and resulting in the continued growth of the charismatic movement. (I prefer the term *caffeinated movement*.)

Youth groups are the worst on this food stuff. I know because I led some. At one church, I had Domino's on speed dial in my cell phone and was on a first name basis with the delivery drivers. I almost bought shares of stock in the company, but I couldn't fit it into my youth budget with all the money we had spent on soft drinks and doughnuts.

The end result is that most preachers are fat and won't tell people to stop eating junk food.

So are the worship leaders and youth leaders and children's leaders and deacons and elders and their wives and husbands and almost everyone else who serves in key positions of influence in the church.

It is a silent epidemic few will address.

Gluttony is the most neglected sin in the American church. If our bodies are the temple of God, then American Christians are the megachurch.

In God's Holy Word, gluttony is listed with all the other taboo issues of our day like good ol' fornication and homosexuality and drunkards and swindlers and people who park in handicapped spaces. But at church, adulterers and homosexuals are easier targets. So are Democrats and Madonna and the emerging/emergent/divergent/submergent church. They're the bad guys (and girls).

And food is fun.

Until you eat too much.

Then it's just sin.

Just like idol worship.

I remember when *American Idol* first became the big show to watch. Pastors didn't like the idea of the word *idol* in the title—me included. Because, as every good Sunday school kid knows, idols are sin.

What every good Sunday school kid does not know is that Jesus was called a big-time sinner for eating too much (along with drinking wine and hanging out with other sinners). Both the Gospels of Matthew and Luke record this. Matthew was a tax collector (translated "major sinner" in first-century Jewish culture) and Luke was a medical doctor. They made certain to carefully note this particular accusation against their Rabbi Master.

So major sinners, from the Jewish perspective, could include an idol worshiper or an overeater.

They're both called sin.

Ouch!

———

But the only person who is likely to call overeating a sin in our churches is a twenty-eight-inch waist guy or a size-zero girl. When he or she does speak out, the average overeater reacts, "But you don't know my situation. It's genetic. Food jumps right into my mouth while I sleep. Burger King is right on the way to work. You don't understand. I have needs!"

But that's beside the point. Is overeating wrong according to Jesus? He made food for 5000 people one time, so I know He *likes* food. But He didn't make French fries or doughnuts. He made fish and bread, two healthy foods. (Interesting note: Jesus was also not vegetarian. He ate fish and lamb on various occasions.)

If I showed up at a church this weekend and they only offered me fish and bread, I would think that was weird. But I'd eat it.

Because that's what Jesus would do.

I think.

———

One church I read about and even visited once upon a time preached a series on physical fitness. It started out this way: The body is God's temple, and we must treat it well to glorify Him and serve as a positive example to others.

All true.

Then the church's leaders grew convicted because they were telling members to maintain a healthy diet but served doughnuts and lots of sugary pastries before and after each service and gave candy to the kids for snacks.

So they decided to do something about it.

They now serve bagels and juice. Krispy Kremes were strictly prohibited.

Go, church!

Of course, the pastor was a skinny guy who played basketball in college, but the point is that he had the courage to take on America's hidden sin of gluttony, including appropriate actions.

But there are some people who eat 12,000 calories a day like Michael Phelps who still don't gain an ounce. For you genetically blessed individuals, please remember that gluttony and overeating is not defined by your dress or waist size. Overeating is a lack of self-control regarding food.

So watch what you eat. Unless your name is Michael Phelps.

Then eat whatever you want because you're the fastest swimmer in the world. And you burn it all off anyway.

And then there's fasting. That's the spiritual practice of not eating food that ministers write bestselling books about. It has nothing to do with speed or winning a race.

And you don't have to be super spiritual or have a PhD in theology and nuclear physics to try it. I personally fast. I go without food for a day at a time on a regular basis to focus on prayer. I don't tell people when I do it or write a book about it or talk about it. I just do it.

But I don't do it for 40 days. Moses and Elijah and Jesus did. Maybe it was part of their training for the Transfiguration or a triathlon or something, but they all had some supernatural help.

One time in college I decided to show God I was really serious and decided to fast until He told me to stop.

Ten and a half days later I started to pass out in my apartment and nearly ended up in the hospital. I took that as God's way of telling me to stop.

I *don't* recommend doing this. In fact, if you've never lived without food for longer than a skipped breakfast, don't get too carried away. Please consult your doctor before fasting. To avoid long-term injury, seek immediate medical attention if you ever feel you have fasted longer than you can safely handle.* Despite possible side effects (both real and imaginary), I'm

---

* Fasting is not for everyone. Individual results may vary. Fasting does not protect against sexually transmitted diseases. The most commonly reported side effects include itchy rashes, paralysis, projectile vomiting, muscle strain, listening to crappy techno music, cramping, full body hair loss, children born with the head of a golden retriever, excessive Calvinism, codependency with inanimate objects, depression, purgatory, extended conversations with socks, demon possession, chain-smoking, interspecies communication, taste loss, UFO sightings, loss of bladder control, speaking in tongues, dandruff, chronic diarrhea, kidney disease, increased gambling, and in rare cases, death.

convinced most Americans eat more food in six days than most people on this planet eat in seven.

Plus, it helps me still fit into the same size of jeans I wore in high school.

If you've read this far into this chapter, you are probably within your ideal weight category or are really interested in this topic or are just really mad at me right now. If you are upset, this is not the goal. The goal is to reintroduce the concept that too much food, just like too much wine or too much work or too much play, is more harmful than helpful.

This is true for your own life and for those you love.

I confess that I love chocolate, ice cream, and Sun Chips, and I sometimes eat them way too much. When I do, I've sinned.

I can acknowledge the fact and seek to improve my bad habits. Or I can pretend it doesn't matter to God how I look on the outside as long as my heart is pure.

But I think God can also see inside my arteries.

Jesus was all about doing life with good food, but all the movies I've seen of Him on the cross include at least a four-pack of abs and sometimes a six-pack. Even Hollywood producers are wise enough to know God wouldn't have a pot belly or man boobs in human form. He would care enough about the food He consumed to control His appetite and be without sin in this area too.

Go and do likewise.

Why I Might Get Fired

Christians like to be right. Some of us get paid to be right.
When we admit we've misrepresented Jesus at some points
along the way, tribal leaders are not always happy.

Non-Christians who really don't like Christians like to mention dirty scandals such as the Crusades or the "Burning Times" or failed predictions for the end of the world. They pick on racism, church leaders caught in adultery, youth pastors who get students pregnant, financial mismanagement, and sexual offenders galore.

In other words, the easy targets.

But when people who call themselves a Christians (like me) highlight complicated issues within the church (like porn or alcohol or homosexuality) and claim to "undefend Christianity," the H-bomb gets dropped.

You already know what the F-bomb is.

But the H-bomb (*heretic*) is even worse for a Christian. To be called a heretic is equal to someone telling me I think Jesus is a myth and the Bible is a cut-and-paste job by the church fathers. A heretic sleeps around and drives a Lexus and listens to NPR.

Note: I'm only guilty of the NPR part.

————

I once knew a guy who was kicked out of his denominational job because he still believed the original statement of faith and wouldn't compromise his beliefs when the rest of the denomination abandoned the faith in a particular area.

Another pastor was told to stop preaching about eternal security (the idea that you can't lose your relationship with God) or be fired.

A third minister was told to quit inviting those public school kids to church or go somewhere else.

That third example was me.

So I left.

Plus, I was tired of singing "Shout to the Lord."

But the main reason was the public school kid thing.

If a lost, let-down, depressed, or brokenhearted person can't be accepted by you and your church family, leave.

I could say it more gently, but I'll save some time and just tell you to straight-up run like heaven.

The church is a group of people committed to sharing Jesus with everyone, regardless of zip code, skin color, IQ, parents, or lack thereof.

But now I write books about how Christianity is the best religion in the world and all the other groups are the bad guys. Then I meet a really nice Muslim professional and feel awkward for slamming the theology he'll hear at his mosque this weekend.

So I'm in this predicament where I believe Jesus is the only way. My passion is to show Christ's compassion to individuals in need and help them experience love and freedom and grace just like I did and still do.

As free people in a free country, we often forget how important freedom really is. In 1845, an American slave named "Aaron" recorded the following story regarding the importance of freedom. To this day, I cannot read it without weeping:

> A poor slave being on his death bed, begged of his master to give him his liberty before he died, "I want to die free, massa." His master replied, "You are going to die soon, what good will your liberty do?" "O master, I want to die free." He said to the slave, "You are free." "But do write it master, I want to see it on paper." At his earnest request he wrote that he was free, the slave took it in his trembling hand, looked at it with a smile and exclaimed, "O how beautiful, O how beautiful," and soon fell asleep in the arms of death.*

---

* This quotation is taken from *The Light and Truth of Slavery: Aaron's History.* The electronic text is available at http://docsouth.unc.edu/neh/aaron/aaron.html. © This work is the property of the University of North Carolina at Chapel Hill. Used by permission.

Sharing this freedom requires speaking the truth, but not without compassion. The apostle Paul called this speaking the truth in love (Ephesians 4:15). That's my target. But what about when Christians argue about how government and public schools are trying to brainwash society and a one-world empire will ultimately kill off all the heathens who don't disappear in the opening scene of the *Left Behind* movie?

They're supposed to be the good guys, but it sure doesn't feel as though that's the case. If I had to choose who to go to lunch with, I'd rather eat with the Muslim who disagrees with me rather than the Christian who is supposed to agree with me but just wants to argue me into his form of fundamentalism.

———

There's this little book out called *The Shack* that a few people have read (like three trillion or so). My first reaction when I read it at Barnes and Noble was that it had nothing to do with Shaq. I had always thought Shaq's biography would be pretty cool. I've often contemplated, "What would life be like as a seven-foot-tall man with lots of money?"

Instead, I got this little book about a guy who goes to a shack and talks with God. Except God looks like Oprah and it doesn't really talk about all the missing gospels or argue that my credit card has something to do with the mark of the beast. It doesn't even include a nuclear Armageddon or include any subplots with an Amish romance.

I was really disappointed. Nobody blew up. There were no terrorists. No car chases. Just a guy in a shack. It's amazing what will pass for a bestseller nowadays.

Then I started talking with other people who had read *The Shack*. Some of the people I spoke with loved it and would almost shed tears in their brief reviews. I thought that was great. Most of the stuff I write makes people cry too, but not for the same reason. I thought I better reread those sections I had skipped to see if I had missed something important like a gruesome beheading or sword fight or cameo by Jack Bauer.

But then some people started telling me about how satanic *The Shack* was. Words such as *occult* and *mysticism* and *Papa John's* were getting thrown around. Some were so angry that I thought even the mention of William P. Young would get me into a fist fight.

I can sympathize with both sides. On the positive side, the book helped some people (apparently a *lot* of people) think about God in a fresh way. On the negative side, the book was somewhat weak (for me) and theologically questionable at points when analyzed via conservative theology.

I'm not about to dissect it here, but my concern was that if *I* started saying some of the stuff I was really thinking about spirituality in our culture, I would help some people along the way...

...but I might also be called a heretic or named Satan's new best friend.

My personal crisis came to a boiling point a couple of years ago. I co-wrote a little book called *Generation Hex* that basically said there are more people into Wicca and witchcraft now than in the past—and Christians should wake up and notice. The idea was to help Christians understand that Wicca was unrelated to Wikipedia or emo or Goth or Elmo or golf and that the best approach was to not be scared but to show love and share your faith as you're able.

Then people started asking me if Oprah was a Christian.

And who I would vote for in the election.

And if Harry Potter was a Christian.

And if I was going to vote for Harry Potter for president.

And if I was working on a book about *Twilight* to confront all of those vampire-loving liberals.

But then some other people started sharing stories about how what I had written or said in an interview had helped them to choose to follow Jesus or start reading the Bible or pray more or talk with a Wiccan without freaking out.

But the people who hated Harry Potter and Oprah and *Twilight* didn't seem to care.

I was mad. Correction, I *am* mad. If a person who claims to follow Jesus wants to call me a heretic because I joke about megachurches and talk to Wiccans and don't boycott Disney, then so be it.

Jesus could go to Disney World and have fun riding on Space Mountain with Oprah and Ellen and a third-degree Wiccan black belt in chai tea latte. You could even throw in William Young and Dan Brown and Don King and Stephen King and Larry King, and Jesus would still be a loving King of kings.

The difference is that He would say He loved each of them and also tell them He has something better in mind for their lives.

They might scoff or reject Him. (Remember, in the New Testament, the influencers killed Him.) But they would at least listen to Him.

Why? Because of love.

Jesus wouldn't be out to debate or hate. He would much rather kick back in a chair with His flip-flops and tell a story than form a political protest of some kind.

In fact, love *is* the greatest protest.

Love protests every form of evil in this world. Jesus did it. He told His followers to do it.

And He's telling *us* to do it.

In the end of the apostle Paul's famous chapter on love in 1 Corinthians 13, he writes, "These three remain: faith, hope and love. But the greatest of these is *love*."

———

Jesus was once asked what the greatest commandment was. His answer was short and sweet. Instead of a list of legalistic statutes no human could ever accomplish, He answered this way: Love God, love people.

Loving God and loving people is my calling as a Christian. And yours (if you are one). So quit blogging about my friendship with Satan and gossiping about the 666 ways I have abandoned the faith by reading about Zen Buddhism so I can share my faith with one of the world's gazillion Buddhists.

I have not left the faith. I'm on your side.

But I am a former fundamentalist.

This means I hate the external junk that blurs the real reasons we love Jesus.

But I still embrace apologetics and theology and the incarnation and gravity and the Trinity and peanut butter and jelly.

I don't like finger painting during worship services, candles that smell girly, Jesus bobble-head dolls, or Bibleman action figures.

And yet I don't start protests over them either.

My only protest sign is this: *Love Jesus More*.

To All the Haters

*A few kind words to those who disagree
with the approach of this book.*

I've had fun making fun of fundamentalists and King James English and Sunday school rooms that look like garage sales after a tornado. In case you haven't picked up on it, I've attempted to inject a fair dose of comedy into some serious Christian situations. If you've been offended by the Holy Spirit, good for you. But if I've offended you by my comments, this is unintentional, and I apologize.

Because my goal is to help people love more, not hate more.

I know a few of you (or maybe a bunch of you) will buy this book just to take out a few quotes to post online or use in your next article or sermon about the emerging church or liberal theology. And while I believe the church should technically be *emerging* (in the sense of *growing*) and that *liberal theology* is an oxymoron on par with *artificial sweeteners*, I do not embrace either movement and cannot in good conscience recommend them to anyone else.

At the same time, many people in these and similar movements have shown far more concern for the poor, the environment, ending sex trafficking, and abolishing modern-day slavery than I have. They're way ahead of me, and I'm doing my best to add solid theology to the mix of social justice. I don't believe the two are mutually exclusive. Contrary to Glenn Beck, *social justice* was part of the plan of Jesus, John the Baptist, and the minor prophets rather than a code word for *socialism*. Jesus and justice can and do go together.

And if you're really interested in my theology, I'm on board with the Apostles' Creed and the Creed of Nicaea, and I occasionally listen to

Creed. I believe modernist theological creeds sometimes say too much while emerging church creeds often say too little.

I believe in one Triune God who is Father, Son, and Holy Spirit, even if I don't completely understand this concept (and you don't either).

I believe Jesus is God in human form who really lived, died, physically rose from the dead, ascended to heaven, and will return for those who place their trust in Him.

I believe the Bible is God's Word. (By this, I mean the 66 books of the Protestant Bible that historically go back to the apostles and Old Testament writers.) It is perfect, and it was originally communicated without error.

I believe the church consists of all individuals of every background who embrace Jesus as Leader and Master of their lives.

I believe we can only know God through Jesus by grace alone through faith alone.

I believe Jesus is coming back, and His children will spend eternity with Him in heaven while those who are not His children will suffer for eternity in hell.

I believe all this, and yet do not speak badly about my nation's president. I attend church regularly with other forgiven sinners like me. I've watched every episode of *Lost*. I love homosexuals even though I am straight. I like coffee. I talk about Jesus whenever I can. I eat at Chili's. I believe *Star Wars* is good for the soul. I pray and read the Bible and give to the poor and eat and drink and love my wife and kids and do everything I can to give glory to God through every action of every day. I am not perfect, and I mess up a lot.

But I'm a work in progress.

And so are you.

I invite you to join me in undefending Christianity.

This world needs more people who care less about their place in history and more about where souls will spend eternity.

We need fewer church building projects and more true church builders.

We need more missionaries to teach the Bible and build homes and feed the hungry and dig wells and stop injustices of every kind.

We need courageous children and teenagers and parents who care more about God's will than their paychecks or popularity and more about God's Word than their next job or what's on TV tonight.

We need you. I need you. Those around the globe who have yet to see the love of Jesus through a human body like yours need you.

So don't let us down.

———

An old friend of mine stopped in town for lunch while traveling back from Florida. He was a student in a ministry where I served 11 years ago. We had a lot of catching up to do.

When I asked him if he was still sharing his faith in Christ with others, he said, "I've shared Jesus with just about everyone I've worked with for the past 12 years. At some of my jobs, my nickname is *Preacher* even though I'm not one."

Would I have ever guessed that students I had served over a decade ago would be sharing Christ across the country, Africa, Australia, Europe, Asia, and Latin America? Sure, I dreamed and prayed it would happen, but to experience it is something quite different. In a word, it is *amazing*.

All across the world today, people like you are pouring their lives into families and small handfuls of students, kids, classmates, and friends to make a difference for eternity. At this moment, you have no idea where your efforts will lead.

In ten years, those you influence will likely be changing lives all around the world. What impact are you making in their lives now that will help them at that time?

Be the change you want to see in this world.

And you'll change yourself and eternity in the process.

Helping Haiti

*On January 12, 2010, the Western Hemisphere's poorest nation
was devastated by an earthquake, that killed more than 200,000
people. I landed in Port-au-Prince 17 days later. This is my story...*

As Christians, we're called to comfort the brokenhearted. But instead, it's a lot easier to comfort ourselves. Maybe we text ten bucks and hope the Red Cross or somebody else will figure it out. Even worse, sometimes we who call ourselves Christians forget that sharing the gospel includes showing up when life falls apart, especially when no one else is there to help.

I began to hear my wake-up call in 2006 after my first trip to Haiti. I returned again less than two years later, prepared to find ways to share my faith and help meet needs in the process. But just a few days into 2010, my plans disappeared as God used one of our generation's worst natural disasters to teach me how Christ's love really looks when all that's left is rubble and pain.

As soon as I heard about the overwhelming earthquake that struck near Port-au-Prince, I began to pray, and I sensed God would have me soon stand on this nation's soil once again. Only 17 days following the initial earthquake, my friend and I arrived in Port-au-Prince, having come on a relief flight with Missionary Flights International.

Under other circumstances, this trip would have made a great vacation. But in this moment, all that was on my mind were the people of Haiti, many of whom had become friends during my previous visits there.

As we flew in, we could see the U.S. military, the UN, Canadian forces, and numerous NGOs (nongovernmental organizations). And we could see some of the destruction—even before landing. However, once we stepped from the plane onto the tarmac, we witnessed the beginning of a much deeper devastation.

First, we walked into what remained of the terminal to meet our contact. His smiling face was a huge relief, as we had few other connections for travel once we had landed. He called for his associate, who was driving a beat-up SUV. We stepped aside for other travelers scrambling toward various relief locations. Some of these workers were coming for only a few days like us; others, such as a team from Canada sharing the flight with us, were staying six months or more. During these few minutes, my friend shot some video, we noticed an array of dangling ceiling tiles, and we wormed our way through the numerous locals who were attempting to carry our bags for a dollar. We passed around some cash for tips, jumped in the vehicle, and snaked through the streets of Port-au-Prince in a daze.

We attempted to video some of the scenes, but between the bumps and the pace of the drive, our clips did little to portray the reality of our surroundings. Building upon building was destroyed. Tents, people, and rubble littered the streets. And while there were no longer bodies along the main roads, many people still wore masks to cover the odor oozing from flattened buildings where unreached bodies decayed.

Forty-five minutes later, our driver pulled up to the gate of Mission of Hope, only three kilometers north of the mass graves containing more than 100,000 corpses trucked from the nearby capital. Yet inside the safety of the mission, a different attitude existed. People still lived in tents, medical emergencies continued to complicate the situation, but the people remained upbeat and positive about what was happening on their 76-acre compound.

We began by dropping off our luggage at the guesthouse and unloading our medical supplies and infant formula at the clinic and the orphanage. My wife, Deborah, had spent hours packing our bags; I wasn't about to fail to get her items immediately into the hands of those who could use them. Intending to start work as soon as possible, we walked downhill toward the warehouse to help. To our surprise, the mission's Haitian team was already unloading an enormous truck of boxed food marked with the word *GAIN*. GAIN was one of the 15-plus NGOs we encountered operating in some way at Mission of Hope after the quake. With no English-speaking workers around, we headed farther downhill toward the clinic, where many volunteers from Austin, Texas had been working.

A few minutes into our orientation, we received a call reporting that U.S. military helicopters had patients on their way. Mission of Hope's clinic, we had been told, was one of only a handful of medical facilities that General Hospital in downtown Port-au-Prince was using to send their massive overflow of patients. Within less than 30 minutes from the time we had arrived, my friend and I were carrying stretchers from helicopters into the clinic for emergency treatment.

I cannot express in words how it feels to sprint up to a roaring chopper, reach out to pick up a stretcher, and realize the person I am picking up is missing a body part. Most of the eight patients flown in that day were amputees or had broken femur bones and had remained untreated for over two weeks. Our medical team instantly began the process of treating amputations for infection, casting broken bones, and providing other necessary services to save the lives of those entrusted to our location.

Of course, the patients flown in via helicopter were not the only ones. Some people were brought in with the clinic's only ambulance, and others came in by truck. Often a few people would just be dropped off at the front gate. That afternoon, a young man who looked about 17 arrived with his left arm missing just below his shoulder. While he was in otherwise excellent physical condition, the earthquake had left its permanent mark on him. His wound was cleaned, pain medication given, and we then moved him to the next building down, an elementary school now converted into what the clinic called "post-op," which was for the care of patients after their initial treatment.

As the sun set that evening, my friend and I joined the other volunteers returning from the region for a meal of gumbo, rice, and water. The table topics ranged from simply food to deeper stuff, such as the number of meals distributed and patient stories from the day.

That evening, I had the opportunity to hang out with some Haitian children. After our meal, they invited me to Friday "movie night," which I found out was a big event at the orphanage. I headed down and watched

Disney's *Cheetah Girls* projected on the side of the orphanage building. The full moon, bright stars, and smiling faces helped me and the 60-plus orphans forget that a spot just down the road held the remains of more people than live in my entire zip code.

One of the highlights of this night for me was the joy of showing love to the children of the orphanage. Though they are well treated and physically fit, many are starved for personal attention, especially from any kind of male father figure. For the entire two-plus hours, I held and hugged little boys and girls, including a baby only a few months old. He loved sucking his thumb and snuggling on my shoulder in the cool night air. I got him to laugh a few times, but soon had to give him up to one of the many preteen girls who enjoyed playing big sister to him.

By the end of the film, one little guy who was about six years old had fallen asleep on the bench with his head on my right leg while I had my left arm around another child who had laughed with her friends throughout the movie. I picked up the little guy and carried him to his house mommy and hopped on the dusty, forest-green four-wheeler for a ride back to the guesthouse.

My friend had passed on movie night and crawled into bed early that evening, overwhelmed both by the events of the day and the lack of any communications—no phones, texting, Internet, or anything! When I took the steps to the second floor, I ran into another volunteer. He had just arrived after driving from Oklahoma to Miami, Florida with tents for a thousand people, purchased through donations given by his home church. He then shipped the tents through DHL to Santo Domingo, flew to the Dominican Republic on a commercial flight, took a bus ride to Mission of Hope, and found his tents arriving about the same time he was. I knew then I had found at least one adventurer just as crazy as I was, and I invited him to stay in our guest room.

————

I awoke to the banging of pans from the Haitian cooks making breakfast downstairs. My phone read 6:37 a.m. Without a real shower in the sense of American plumbing, I washed off in the bathtub faucet, changed clothes, and walked downstairs to join the other awakening relief workers. Some volunteers were headed to the airport to leave for the U.S. and

Canada; others were on their way in later that evening. A few of us were assigned to sort medical supplies in the warehouse because the Haitian workers would not be able to read the French, English, and sometimes-German-and-Spanish labels on the products. I could decipher the labels, another knew what the products were, and my friend moved pallets and labeled them for easy access.

By late morning, we were almost finished sorting 31 pallets of medical supplies that had been shipped from Austin (over 26,000 pounds' worth) when we again heard the familiar sound of a U.S. military chopper approaching. We ran to the clinic, where we carried the stretchers of more amputee and broken-femur patients into the triage area. One helicopter turned into two, and then two turned into three. In total, we transported about eight patients and their family members. On the last drop-off, one military officer asked the name of our location, to which I responded, "Mission of Hope." I guessed that he appreciated the expertise of the medical volunteers at our clinic, and he was probably pleased that we carried all those patients' stretchers. Perhaps he wanted to keep us in mind for future flights. I later discovered this was exactly the case.

The remainder of that Saturday was a blur. We helped move amputees from stretchers to beds, from beds to their operations, and from their operations onto either the ambulance or a delivery truck. The truck would move them into the post-op school building for recovery. At one point, I helped two other guys put five different people who were either on stretchers or in wheelchairs into a delivery truck, because our ambulance was busy taking a different patient to another hospital. The truck was all that was available, and new patients needed their space. Ironically, this was also the same exact truck I had ridden to the airport when leaving Haiti the summer before. At that time, I had been praying that God would use me to help in Haiti in the future. He had answered my prayer.

That night, I listened to every story I could at the dinner area. Doctors talked about their surgeries. Relief workers coordinated efforts for the next day's deliveries. A filmmaker shared stories of the footage he had captured in the capital: He had caught a riot breaking out during food distribution and discussions from a meeting of NGOs in the capital. News spread regarding American missionaries who were arrested attempting to traffic children across the border. At that point, few knew the details or the seriousness of this event, which would make the international news for weeks to follow. Everyone was tired. No one complained.

The next morning, Sunday, was church. With the exception of the night-shift nurses who had stayed up until sunrise with patients following their operations, everyone attended the service. It was a much-needed break and spiritually necessary for many of the believers who had given so unselfishly of their lives since coming to Haiti.

Hope Church typically has about 500 people in an open-air building for its two-hour time of worship. This particular morning had over 700 worshipers. Most were under 18, including several young kids who swarmed around my friend and me either out of curiosity or in hopes of making a dollar. The service itself was amazing. At the keyboard, the worship leader played many American Christian tunes using Haitian Creole lyrics, though an occasional chorus in English or French popped up to involve the volunteers who were attending.

I had been practicing some Creole ever since my last trip to Haiti the previous June, but I was limited to a few words and phrases during this trip until the worship service. The church used an LCD projector with the lyrics to the songs, which allowed me to sing along in Creole, praising God in the local language in a very real and moving way.

At the end, to the surprise of many, about 12 people walked up to the pastor when he asked congregants to do so if they would like to become Christians. Even he looked amazed at the response. In Haitian style, they asked the new converts to kneel in a time of prayer. An enormous cheer arose from the audience after the final "amen," and these men and women started a new life in the middle of one of the most challenging times in Haiti's history.

Afterward, I wrestled off kids begging for money and candy after giving everything in my backpack away, and I began walking toward the clinic. Just then, a young man stopped me. His name was James. He was the brother of my translator from the previous summer, Philip. We had been trying to connect, but we had kept missing each other due to poor cell phone coverage in the area. I was able to chat for about ten minutes and leave a small financial gift I had brought for him and Philip's family. James had with him another brother of his and Philip's and one other friend who spoke a little English. All three men were in their twenties. I was excited to spend a few moments with some of Haiti's young leaders who reminded me a lot of the students I mentor back in the States.

But then it happened again—another helicopter. I said my goodbyes and sprinted up the hill with my backpack bouncing each step of the way. As I reached the clinic, the first chopper circled and landed. I dropped my pack and sprinted to the first stretcher, where I found a young man with a missing foot being transported along with his father.

Two additional helicopters arrived shortly afterward, creating a near-frantic scene for many of the volunteers just starting work after the worship service. No one had eaten, and the volunteers were still preparing beds with sheets when I and another person arrived carrying the first stretcher.

The original plan had been to eat lunch, see what work needed to be done, and then head into Port-au-Prince with our translator. Two friends and I wanted to check out the damages around the city to assess future work needs.

However, now everyone was moving quickly to keep up with the on-the-spot medical operations. After each surgery, I helped move patients to post-op, returning each time to assist with the next need. On one of my last runs, I saw a teenage girl weeping at the front entrance of the clinic. One of the mission's leaders stood beside her. I asked what had happened and discovered her dad had just died. He had been brought in with a broken leg, with the bone sticking out. As they prepared to treat him, his heart stopped beating before the operation could even begin. The doctors believed he had a blood clot that had caused his sudden death. But I could only stay a few minutes before being called to transport another patient sitting in a wheelchair.

———

It was 4:00 p.m. before the new team of volunteers from Austin had everything under control and we were down to only a few remaining operations for the evening. The three of us and our translator finally jumped into a road-worn burgundy Cherokee and exited the gate for the first time since our arrival.

We first stopped at the mass grave just south of Mission of Hope near Titanyen. The earthmovers were not in operation that day, so we expected to simply walk around, pray, and snap a few pictures to say we had been there.

I noticed an area that had not been covered up. I thought a shot of an empty hole would be a nice addition to our collection of footage and proceeded to walk toward it with my flip video recorder in hand. Getting nearer, I spotted something brown in front of a mound of rubble. At first, I dismissed the idea that it could really be a body. Those would have all been buried by now.

But as I got even closer, the unmistakable smell of death rushed through my nostrils. I had seen dead bodies before, but I was not prepared for the lump of decaying flesh at my feet from an earthquake that had happened over two weeks ago. Today was January 31. Nineteen days had passed since the 7.0 earthquake that had started this tragedy. My friend yelled at me to stop, but I had already seen the rotting corpse by that point. I veered to the right as soon as the odor hit, shielding my face from the putrid stench.

I returned speechless across the rubble that covered more than 100,000 people, their remains just below the very rocks on which I was walking. A biblical concept came to mind: "Mourn with those who mourn."

The rest of our drive through the capital and surrounding area only heightened my grief. At first, I was in an odd way excited to capture photos and footage of flattened buildings. But after about 20 minutes of crushed structures, one after another, I was left stunned. What I had experienced in my original trip from the airport was only a portion of the destruction. Much of the capital city lay in ruins.

No place illustrated this devastation better than the scene outside the presidential palace. Haiti's equivalent of the American White House had collapsed. The entire building resembled a giant pancake. At that point we stepped out of our vehicle onto the sidewalk alongside another film crew, where we felt the safety of numbers near the sprawling tent city behind us.

Here I experienced other smells—ones I will not soon forget. They were smells of the living…food, urine, and excrement. They were all mixed together among the voices of thousands of souls living in conditions I would not wish on my worst enemy.

We spotted completely naked people bathing in buckets of water. Children urinated on the sidewalk only steps away from where we stood. Most men and women simply walked around staring hopelessly, not certain if they would live to see another day.

From there, we headed back to the mission, but not before driving through Cité Soleil, the poorest slum in the poorest country in the Western Hemisphere. Our translator drove quickly through this area, admitting that he had been carjacked in this neighborhood several years ago. It was mostly a multi-acre field of rusted corrugated metal shacks and tarps supported by sticks. We spotted only one water truck—mobbed by a line of bucket-carrying women who were hoping to survive another evening in the most extreme poverty imaginable.

We arrived at Mission of Hope just as the sun was setting, a gorgeous blend of yellow, orange, and gold hues over the waters of the Caribbean. Too shocked to process all I had seen, heard, and smelled during the daylight hours, I ate little and conversed only briefly that evening, then packed for our departure the next morning. My last thoughts of the night were simply, "God, heal this land."

———————

Monday morning, day four of our time in Haiti, was to be the day of our return. The three of us ended up flying on a U.S. military C-130 transport. We gave our fingerprints, signed some waivers, and sat with about 40 other Americans to wait for the next flight. It turned out they were heading to Orlando. Orlando was 90 minutes from the car of one of my friends in Fort Pierce, far better than JFK in New York, where some other planes had been traveling.

———————

We landed at Orlando-Sanford Airport a few hours later in a heavy downpour. After passing through immigration, the three of us headed to the car rental area, trying three companies before finding an available car.

At the last minute, a guy named Bill told us his car was at the same agency in Fort Pierce we were driving to, and he joined us for the ride. Our first stop was McDonalds.

The other guys in the car were excited about getting some American fast food. I could still barely eat, but got a little something so I didn't look too weird. I still had dust on my shoes from our visit to the mass grave yesterday.

By 2:30 a.m. Tuesday morning, day five of the journey, we had all said our goodbyes, and I was crawling into bed beside my wife after my first hot shower in a week. While I was thankful to be home, as I drifted off to sleep my mind continued to replay the tragedies and the changed lives I had witnessed.

I know for certain I am no longer the same person I was. What remains to be seen is what God will do following the time I have spent there. After this third journey to the nation, I have a list full of phone numbers and contacts in Haiti. People are e-mailing and calling me regularly about help with more recovery efforts. And all I want to do is return. I'm not sure what this means, but God does, and I plan to keep following Him each step of the way, whether it involves helping from my laptop and mobile phone or going back again and again until God's plan for me in Haiti is complete.

That Jesus

Because Jesus is only Jesus if we're really talking about Jesus.

I've been sick this week, which means I lie awake at night and think more than usual.

I've also been reading *The Message* and Donald Miller while listening to vintage U2 and taking Advil, a combination that really changes a person's perspective.

All that said, I've been really thinking about one of my biggest frustrations with American Christianity. My frustration is that people don't say what they're really thinking. I ask, "How are you?" and the person says, "Fine." It doesn't matter if the guy just filed for divorce or won the lottery. It's always, "Fine."

When I talk to homeless people on the street, they never say fine. I ask, "How are you?" and they just start talking. Sometimes I have no idea what they're talking about, but at least they tell me.

If many Christians were really honest, they would just skip waiting for an answer and say, "How are you? Great, me too. See you later. God bless."

But what if we really did care how people were doing? What if instead of code words such as *fine* and *great*, we stopped to talk about real issues, real problems, and even the *S* word—sin?

But that would be too real. Too revealing. It's easier to pretend.

To wear the mask.

When I was a kid, I dressed up like Darth Vader one year for Halloween. When I put on the dark helmet, I *was* Darth Vader. I could wield a red lightsaber, command storm troopers, and had a son I was trying to convince to join the dark side and rule the galaxy with me. It didn't matter that I was six. All that mattered was that I was wearing the mask.

147

American Christianity is a lot like me wearing that Darth Vader mask. I put on my mask and act the part, even if I'm someone completely different inside. Why do we do this?

There are lots of reasons, but they're different for each person. Fear. Pride. Fatigue. Being told a thousand times not to let people see the real you. But these reasons are all paths that lead back to one source. The source at the end of these broken roads is insecurity.

The mask offers security. I wouldn't ask you to join the dark side of the force in a pair of khakis and a polo shirt. But I could do it in a Darth Vader mask.

Why can't we take off our masks as followers of Christ? The Bible says to confess our sins to one another to be healed. The same Book tells us to pray for one another, encourage one another, and help one another.

But that would be too simple. Doing what God says.

Or would it?

Sometimes I think the most difficult things in the world to do are the simple things. Like taking out the trash. How hard could that be? But I can think of 529 other things I'd rather do when I can't close the lid to our metal kitchen trash can, the kind with the fancy foot pedal where you don't have to actually touch the stuff you put inside. So instead, I keep pushing the dinner leftovers down deeper and deeper.

Then my wife gets angry. Then I take out the trash.

Because we sleep together at night and I don't like to go to bed with my wife angry at me.

If I lived alone, I would be in big trouble because the trash would only get taken out when it started blocking the doorway.

But pushing the trash down deeper is what comes naturally, whether in my kitchen or in my everyday life. Nobody wants to see my trash or deal with it. They want "Fine."

Only Jesus *really* wants to deal with our trash. And the only people who want to help me with my trash are the people who are really trying to be like Jesus.

Which is why I keep wondering why people at church wear masks. And like "Fine." And don't like to take out the trash.

Like *me*. I'm guilty too. Life is short, and I'd rather spend it on myself than listening to someone whine about their boss or mortgage or roommate.

Except for that part of me that wants to be more like Jesus. That part really wants to sit down over a cup of steaming coffee and listen to every little issue in the lives of people I would normally just end the conversation with after "Fine."

Because that's what Jesus does with me.

Jesus listens. He knows "Fine" isn't the truth. He knows all about my mask. And my trash. And He still listens.

This fascinates me. Not that Jesus knows these things. If Jesus is God, then He knows everything. What I find staggering is that He knows everything about me and still wants to spend time with me.

I want to be more like Jesus. Not the bobble-head Jesus or the "Jesus is my homeboy" or the What-Would-Jesus-Do Jesus, but the Jesus that Matthew and Mark and Luke and John write about. The Jesus who left His Dad to spend time with blue-collar workers and corrupt financial investors and prostitutes and homeless people. And me.

I want to be more like that Jesus.

ABOUT THE AUTHOR

Dillon Burroughs is an activist and bestselling author of nearly 30 books on issues of faith and culture. He has served among at-risk American youth, constructed housing in Mexico's barrios, provided aid relief in Haiti, and was most recently nominated for a CNN Hero award for his efforts to fight human trafficking. His written and edited works have been featured by NPR, MSNBC, ABC News, and other media outlets.

www.readDB.com

Acknowledgments

Acknowledgments are the place in a book where the writer is supposed to thank the people who helped him make the book possible. This includes God, everyone I've ever met, everyone who has helped edit, publish, and sell my books, and all of you who will read my words at some point in the next half century, especially if you blog, mention it on talk radio or TV, send me a gift card, or even give me a ninja invite on Facebook.

Now that I've covered everybody, let me name some individuals who stand out as I wrap up these final words: First, my wife, Deborah, and my kids Ben, Natalie, and Audrey. You are why I get up at ungodly hours to do godly work so I can drive home early enough to rub feet, build Legos, play My Little Pony, and change diapers. (Shout out: You can already begin viewing the works of my eight-year-old son Ben at BenjaminBurroughs.com. Check it out.)

To my praying friends and family—Dorothy, my mom, The DeShong-Martin tribe, the Burroughs fam, the Ankerberg team, everyone at Woodland Park, White River, Sherman Bible, Ridgedale Baptist, Fellowship Bible Dallas, Northcrest, FBCNTH (you know who you are), Agape Fellowship, and Deer Creek.

My publishing buddies—Bob Hawkins Jr., Ben Hawkins, Terry Glaspey, LaRae Weikert, Paul Gossard, the individuals I met with in sales and marketing, and the rest of the team at Harvest House. CBA, ECPA, NRB, and bookstores everywhere, especially all the indie booksellers who have helped so many in their communities. To Joel and the team at Alive, you are simply the best.

My barista friends at Hamilton Place.

To the outstanding servants at Compassion International, Mercy Movement, Home of Hope Texas, Freeset Global, Project Rescue, ALERT, WorldCrafts, MTM Haiti, and Mission of Hope Haiti: You show Christ's love like few others in this world. I always wish I could do more. I'll keep doing what I can.

To Christina Mackenzie, Brant Hansen, Mark and Sandra Palmer, and Charles Powell: Thank you for sharing your stories as part of my story in these pages. You are the true heroes of the faith.

My unofficial soundtrack, including music from Switchfoot, The Fray, Addison Road, Coldplay, Chris Tomlin, U2, and the David Crowder Band.

To every reader of these words who longs to follow Jesus no matter the cost, both near and far, from every tongue, tribe, nation, and denomination: Thank you for exploring spirituality with me through the highs and lows of humanity that speak the truth and point to *the* truth of Jesus, whether popular where you live or not. I pray for you daily.

And to Nick Jr., Lego, Hasbro, and the makers of videos and toys for my kids: They're fun even if they cost way too much.

Crave
Chris Tomlinson

People yearn for many things, but only Jesus Christ can satisfy the deepest cravings of the human heart. Many individuals, however, have settled for a cultural Christianity and lost their vibrant, day-by-day relationship with Him. This collection of short, real-life stories from an exciting young author reveals that your life with God can be a surprising, challenging, and richly satisfying journey.

Sometimes humorous, occasionally tender, and always thought-provoking, these slices of life will connect with you if you crave a deeper level of intimacy with God.

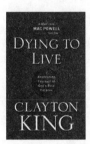

Dying to Live
Abandoning Yourself to God's Bold Paradox
Clayton King

Do you want to *live*? Do want to be sold out to something that will outlive you and outlast your existence? Then you have to die. It's the only way to gain life. The only way to fill that deep-inside longing. The only way to really know Christ—because it's *His* way.

International speaker and evangelist Clayton King shares 20 bold pictures from Scripture, his own life, and the lives of others that will

- make you sick of existing just to get more stuff, money, and "success"
- grip your soul with longing for the life Jesus promised
- stir up your passion for God's mission to build a kingdom that will last forever

It's a reality that's no longer about you.

> *"You wake up to a world filled with colors and tastes and textures and conversation and songs and laughter, a world that no longer revolves around your own petty drama but around God's bigger story of rebuilding what we have all broken."*

The Compassion Revolution
Dave Donaldson, with Terry Glaspey

Jesus fed the hungry. He touched the outcasts and the unlovable. He healed the sick and lame. He forgave those tormented by guilt. Jesus was a compassion revolutionary.

Dave Donaldson, cofounder of Convoy of Hope and himself a compassion revolutionary, urges you to join him in responding to the call of Jesus to visibly demonstrate the radical values of the kingdom of God.

The Compassion Revolution is filled with stories that will inspire you to align your priorities with God's plan for living an extraordinary life. It is an invaluable guide to encourage you to live a purposeful, fulfilled, and enriched life that comes only by giving it away to others.

Sex, Food, and God
Breaking Free from Temptations, Compulsions, and Addictions
David Eckman

The good things created by God, like food and sex, can be misused to run away from emotional/relational pain. When this happens, the damage and loneliness can be worse than the worst nightmare. Using groundbreaking research and offering compassionate understanding rooted deeply in the Bible, David Eckman shares

- how and why unhealthy appetites grip and trap people in a fantasy world

- how shame and guilt disappear when we realize how much God delights in us

- how four great experiences of the spiritual life break the addiction cycle

> "David Eckman is a man you can trust...His teaching resonates with God's wisdom and compassion."

—**Stu Weber,** author of *Tender Warrior*

To learn more about other Harvest House books
or to read sample chapters, log on to our website:

www.harvesthousepublishers.com

HARVEST HOUSE PUBLISHERS
EUGENE, OREGON